MW00901142

KETO EASY LASY

The Complete Keto Cookbook with
Easy-to-Follow and Quick-to-Make Recipes
21-Day Meal Plan for a Quick Weight Loss
Easy Shopping List for Effortless Results

Bronson Duncan

Copyright © 2019 by Bronson Duncan

All rights reserved worldwide.

ISBN: 978-1699804858

No part of this book may be reproduced or transmitted in any form or by any means, electronic or mechanical, including photocopying, recording or by any information storage and retrieval system, without written permission from the publisher, except for the inclusion of brief quotations in a review.

Warning-Disclaimer

The purpose of this book is to educate and entertain. The author or publisher does not guarantee that anyone following the techniques, suggestions, tips, ideas, or strategies will become successful. The author and publisher shall have neither liability or responsibility to anyone with respect to any loss or damage caused, or alleged to be caused, directly or indirectly by the information contained in this book.

CONTENTS

INTRODUCTION

If you're reading this book, the chances are that you have heard about all the "miracles" of the keto diet, but you don't exactly know how to pull it off.

Or you might be struggling to come up with some new, delicious recipes to enrich your meal plan. That's great! I've been there and done that. This book will not only make you salivate over yummy recipes you'll discover in this book. It will also be your gateway to starting and adopting a keto-diet lifestyle forever.

No matter what occasion, no matter your taste - you'll find plenty of simple recipes to get you in better shape and flat out to improve your health. You don't have to eat like a monk just because you want to quit carbs. With those recipes, you'll be able to keep eating mouth-watering food while slimming down your body.

The Keto diet has been around for more than nine decades now. You can go on it regardless of your age or type of body you have. It's been proven countless times to work well for all groups of people.

Even though the list of "forbidden" food items can scare some of you off, in reality, it offers lots of very easy swaps. And with all those alternatives, you can be as creative as you want! Sky... I mean...your fantasy is the limit!

WELCOME TO THE KETO LIFESTYLE

There's a common misconception that the human body has to run on carbohydrates. That they are the best source of energy for us to function correctly. What few people know, however, is that carbohydrates are just one way to go to provide ourselves with enthusiasm, but not the only one.

Our bodies are such complex machines that we can create energy from alternative sources such as as...fats. The process where we run low on carbs and our body is forced to "switch" too fat is the beginning of what we call ketosis.

Contrary to what many people think, the ketogenic diet is not some modern-day fancy invention promoted by the mainstream to sell more books or certain foods. Its beginning dates back to the 1920s, and this diet has since then provided hundreds of testimonials of its amazing effects.

If you happen to be new to this topic, let me perhaps take a step back to avoid your confusion. To understand the idea of the ketogenic diet, it's good for you also to understand the "big picture," which in that case, means what happens in your body when you eat carbs.

Let's say you have just devoured a big bowl of spaghetti. You're full to the brim, you've got your dopamine kick, and you feel happy. You just gave your body an extra-large carbo-gift. So as soon as you're done with eating, your digestive system starts to work at full capacity. And this is when the magic happens. Carbohydrates are broken down in the digestive process, and they turn to glucose, our cells' fuel. This is where your energy comes from.

You may want to ask, "what's the problem with those carbs anyway?" Well, there are a few things you should know if you're going to eat consciously and pick the right food. The biggest of all the culprits are undoubtedly sugar-level spikes. Carbohydrates increase your blood sugar more than any other nutrient out there. And in the long run, it's dangerous because it heightens the risk for your body to develop diabetes. Another issue with carbs is that when the blood sugar drops again, you may experience an energy crash. And of course, you'll end up grabbing another meal or a snack way faster.

They're much like having a hot romance. It's intense, but it ends quickly and is often not worth it. So, how is the keto diet a better alternative to how you eat now?

Well, the main difference, of course, is that you change the proportions of nutrients you eat. You reduce carbohydrates in no small degree, you keep proteins moderate, and you guessed it right - you add a whole lot of fats. So now, when there are barely any carbs left, your body, to produce energy, is forced to source it from somewhere else. And because your body, to some degree, consists of fat, the liver will start using it as an energy source. As a result of that, your body weight will begin to decrease.

How to enter the state of Ketosis

The Ketosis is started when your liver starts the process of breaking down fat that's present in there. As a result of that, molecules called ketones are being created. Ketones are what glucose is for the carbs. That means they're a result of the digestion process, and you can think of them as energy particles. This is also where the name "ketogenic" comes from.

The controversy that makes many people skeptical about this diet is the process of switching from glucose to ketones. Some think that this process can threaten their bodies. The reality, however, is that this is an entirely safe process, and your body won't be impacted in any negative way from the switch. It may come as a bit of "shock" for your body, but it's far from being dangerous. All it takes to adapt is just giving it some time. But as with everything, isn't it so?

The adaptation phase can vary on a case-by-case basis. There are no fixed rules for everyone.

In most cases, however, it takes about two weeks to become accustomed to the new diet. After all, you've been passionately eating carbs, most likely all your life. So no panic, let your body do its job, and it'll all take care of itself.

A handful of tips to get you started

Cut back on carbs - the biggest obstacle for most people. But it's necessary if you aim at having results. The ideal scenario would be keeping the carbs under the level of 30-40g per day. The 21-Day Meal Plan you'll find in this book will help you keep the ketosis state all the time. Every day is set to prevent your daily intake below 20g of net carbs. That is for all meals counted together.

Limit Proteins - too much of proteins, and you can disturb the ketosis process. Ideally, you should aim at 20-25% of your calories coming from proteins.

Drink Water - the core element of all diets and an overall healthy lifestyle. Water will help you control hunger pangs by filling your stomach. It is also crucial in regulating many body functions that can work in a bit different way when you start the diet. A rule of thumb would be to go with 3 liters a day.

Intermittent Fasting - what few people know, fasting is a handy tool to lift the ketones levels permanently. This method works as long as your lifestyle lets you stay without food for periods no shorter than 12 hours. There are many ways to go about intermittent fasting, and it can last anything from 12 to 20 hours of daily fasting or more extended periods like 24-upwards but repeated less frequently. The most popular fasting-system is arguably 16 hours of fast with 8 hours left for eating throughout the day.

Get Moving - "A healthy mind in a healthy body," as the saying goes. This is true even more when you're on a keto diet. Try to have at least 30 minutes of exercise every day. If, for some reason, it's hard to accomplish, stick to a thirty-minute walk to stimulate your metabolism and balance your blood sugar level. Besides, this will put you in a state of feeling "invincible," so every goal or discipline will seem more natural to accomplish. Plus, all kinds of temptations will appear to be "against" your efforts, so you'll be much less likely to indulge in compulsive carb-eating behavior.

How to tell if you're in the ketosis state

In the beginning, you may find it difficult to know if you're already in the ketosis stare or not. That's normal; most people struggle with it in the beginning.

Luckily, there are ways to deal with it. Common symptoms of being in the state of ketosis are, for example, dry mouth, increased urination, reduced hunger, and an overall feeling of having more energy (this is thanks to low blood sugar level). Another way to tell if you're in the ketosis state is by blood stips. This option, contrary to the first one, involves spending some money. The last but by all means, the most precise method is using a device called Precision Xtra by the company Abbott. It measures the glucose and blood levels of BHP (beta-hydroxybutyrate). The minimum threshold is at least 0.7 mmol. For a deeper state of ketosis, you should be aiming at anything between 1 and 3 mmol.

Side Note for Fasting: If you are planning on going on a 2-5-day fast (that is not consuming any calories at all), you should research some additional ketone supplementation plus it is advisable to increase the consumption of vitamins and amino acids. For more specific and individual support, you may want to consult with your doctor.

THE KETO-BENEFITS

From losing some extra kilos to enhancing longevity, there are many advantages of introducing the keto diet to your life.

Loss of Appetite

If opening your fridge five minutes after you've decided that you don't need anything from there sounds familiar to you - don't worry. That may be one of the signs that you should try switching to the keto diet. It will help you refuse this other portion of pasta, fries, or candies. As soon as your body becomes accustomed to producing its "fuel" from fats instead of carbs, you should see an immediate drop in your appetite.

Weight Loss

When the level of glucose is low, so is the level of insulin as your liver doesn't have to produce it to counter the effect of the increased glucose level. As a result of that, your kidneys will start removing the extra sodium from the body. Next thing you'll know will be losing weight.

HDL Cholesterol Increase

One of the very desired outcomes of being on keto-diet is the rise of the so-called "good cholesterol" - HDL. This means that your veins and arteries will remain unclogged, healthy, and by the same token, you'll slash the risk of developing many cardiovascular diseases.

Drop-in Blood Pressure

Reducing carbohydrates in your diet will also help you normalize your blood pressure. That is key in prevention against heart diseases and heart strokes.

Lower Risk of Diabetes

Although the mechanism is rather distinct, it's worth stressing it even more. This is in a direct link to the fact that carbohydrates that trigger glucose production are reduced in the digestion process. This means less burden for your liver that continually has to produce insulin to balance the effect of glucose.

Improved Brain Function

According to different studies, fat is an energy source that vastly enhances mental clarity and improves brain functions. "A healthy mind in a healthy body."

Longevity

This benefit is linked to lowering the levels of oxidative stress in your body. It has been scientifically proven that once this happens, the lifespan gets extended as well. So...long live the keto-diet!

A TYPICAL KETO-PLATE

Contrary to what you may believe, being on a ketogenic diet doesn't mean any torturous food regime. It doesn't mean sticking to some tight schedule of meals either. You can eat as many times as you want. The only thing to concentrate on is the balance of fats vs. proteins and carbohydrates. Specifically, you should stick to the following proportions:

65-75 % Fat

20-30 % Protein

5-10 % Carbohydrates

As a rule of thumb, you shouldn't eat more than 20 grams of NET carbs a day. That is the total carbs minus fiber and sugar alcohols (erythritol, xylitol, etc.)

That's regardless if you eat it all at once or divided into tiny portions. If you think that's not possible to reach 20 grams of net carbs, don't worry, you'll find such recipes in this book. Some of them will not contain any net carbs at all, some of them just a few grams.

KETO-FLU

This is something that couldn't be just skipped in this introduction. In the beginning, some people experience symptoms that can look and feel a bit like flu. The good news is that it disappears as quickly as it appears. Usually, a week is enough for it to pass by. So typical symptoms of the "keto flu" are feeling fatigued, headache, nausea, or even cramps.

The reason why the flu can happen to any newbie is two-fold:

- **The diuretic effect of the diet:** it translates to visiting the bathroom more often, which in turn causes a loss of electrolytes and water. To prevent it, you can drink more water or a bouillon cube. This will help replenish electrolytes necessary to function well. Additionally, you can increase the consumption of potassium, magnesium, calcium, and phosphorus.

- **The shock-effect.** Since our bodies are designed to source the energy from carbs, it may come as a shock to your body when there is almost none. That's why you will probably experience fatigue or even nausea. The solution for that would be not to go cold turkey when switching to fats. Instead, try to do it gradually. This is easier with the 21-Day Meal Plan you can find in this book. To facilitate the transition, the recipes for the first few days will contain slight amounts of carbs.

WHAT TO EAT

Certain foods will help you heighten your fat intake and make sure your energy level is high over the next hours (that's because the energy from fats is being released slower than the one from carbs) So consider choosing from the following options:

- Meats

- Eggs

- Fish and Seafood

- Bacon, Sausage

- Cacao and sugar-free chocolate

- Avocado and berries

- Leafy Greens - all of them

- Vegetables: cucumber, zucchini, asparagus, broccoli, onion, brussel sprout, cabbage, tomato, Eggplant, seaweed, peppers, squash

- Full-Fat Dairy (heavy cream, yogurt, sour cream, cheese, etc.)

- Nuts — they're a valuable source of healthy fats, but you have to take more caution if you want to eat pistachios, chestnuts, or cashews. They contain more carbs than the rest. The best option to stay keto are Macadamia nuts, walnuts, pecans, and almonds.

- Seeds - chia, flaxseed, sunflower seeds

- Sweeteners - stevia, erythritol, xylitol, monk fruit sugar. I use mostly stevia and erythritol. The latter is a sugar alcohol, but it doesn't spike blood sugar thanks to its zero glycemic indexes.

- Milk - consume full-fat coconut milk or almond milk

- Flour - coconut or almond flour and almond meal

- Oils - olive oil, avocado oil

- Fats - butter or ghee

- Salt - pink Himalayan salt or sea salt

WHAT TO SAY GOODBYE TO

If you want to stay on track with your diet, there are certain things that you need to avoid. It may not be easy at the beginning, but after a week or two, you should start adapting to your new menu. The list includes food items like:

- Sugar, honey, agave

- Diet soda, sugary drinks, and fruit juices

- Starchy Vegetables such as potatoes, beans, legumes, peas, yams, and corn are usually packed with tons of carbs, so they must be avoided. However, sneaking some starch when your daily carb limit allows, is not exactly a sin.

- Flour - all-purpose flour, wheat flour, cornflour, rice flour

- Dried fruits and fruit in general, except for berries

- Grains — rice, wheat, and everything made from grains such as pasta or bread are not allowed.

- Margarine or Milk

- Refined Oils and Fats (corn oil, canola oil, vegetable oil, etc.)

KETO SWAPS

Although eating rice or pasta is not allowed, it doesn't mean that you cannot enjoy a risotto or spaghetti anymore. Well, in a way. Thankfully, there something called keto-swaps, which means that for almost every traditional item on the "forbidden list," there's a keto-equivalent for it. And they're all delicious! So here's the list:

Bread and Buns - Bread made from nut flour, mushroom caps, cucumber slices

Wraps and Tortillas - Wraps and tortillas made from nut flour, lettuce leaves, kale leaves

Pasta and Spaghetti - Spiralized veggies such as zoodles, spaghetti squash, etc.

Lasagna Noodles - Zucchini or eggplant slices

Rice - Cauliflower rice (ground in a food processor)

Mashed Potatoes - Mashed Cauliflower or other veggies

Hash Browns - Cauliflower or Spaghetti squash

Flour - Coconut flour, Hazelnut flour, Almond Flour

Breadcrumbs - Almond flour, Pork rinds

Pizza Crust - Crust made with allowed flour, Cauliflower crust

French Fries - Carrot sticks, Turnip fries, Zucchini fries

Potato Chips - Zucchini chips, Kale chips

Croutons - Bacon bits, nuts, sunflower seeds, flax crackers

TRADITIONAL HIGH CARB COMFORT FOODS MADE KETO

Bagel 1 plain 50g net carbs → Low-Carb or FatHead Bagel 1 plain 4.8g net carbs

Bread 1 slice 12g net carbs → Keto Bread - 1 slice 1.5g net carbs

Risotto 1 cup 40g net carbs → Cauliflower Risotto 1 cup 4g net carbs

Mashed Potatoes 1 cup 30g net carbs → Mashed Cauliflower 1 cup 5g net carbs

Roasted Potatoes 1 cup 20g net carbs → Roasted Radishes 1 cup 4.2g net carbs

Pasta 1 cup 40g net carbs → Zoodles/Shirataki Noodles 1 cup 3.8g/1.2g net carbs

Pepperoni Pizza 1 slice 23g net carbs → Cheesy Bell Pepper Pizza 3.7g net carbs

Waffle 1 waffle 17g → Keto Waffle 1 waffle 4.8g net carbs

HOW TO GET STARTED BROKEN DOWN TO 5 STEPS

1. **The big clean-up** - get rid of all pasta, rice, bread, potatoes, corn, wraps, sugary foods, drinks, legumes, fruits, etc. The less you're exposed to these foods, the less likely you will reach for them to satisfy your craving.

2. **Redesign your food stock** - now it's time to replace the removed items. Go for great shopping and follow the tips from the previous lists.

3. **Prepare Your Kitchen** - consider equipping your kitchen with a few handy helpers if you don't yet have them. The following list will make your life significantly easier:

    - food scales

    - a blender/food processor

    - hand mixer

    - cast iron pans

    - baking dish

    - heatproof bowls

    - spiralizer

The recipes from this book will mainly be based on using these devices in different configurations. So think of them, not as expenses but rather investments that will help you achieve your goals and become a better version of yourself. They will be your friends.

4. **Meal Plan** - planning your meals upfront will make it more comfortable for you to maintain the discipline. I especially recommend it to all those who start their keto-journey. And that's precisely why my team and I developed a complete 21-Day Meal Plan. If you stick to it, everything should go smoothly.

5. **Exercise** - the human body is designed to move always. I understand that it's hard when you're tired, but the movement is going to give you additional leverage. You'll see that it's just easier to stick to healthier habits when your brain rewards you with dopamine after complete training. You want to keep yourself in this good mood, and cheating on carbs would ruin it in a glimpse. Any anaerobic activity will be excellent - jogging, running, bicycling, or even walking for at least 30 minutes a day. You don't have to limit yourself to anaerobic exercises. Some additional strength training would also be a significant benefit to your body; however, I suggest you consult a professional personal trainer about it.

GOING OUT ON A KETO DIET

You may find cooking at home an ordeal and a waste of time waste, but this is key in not giving in to temptation when you're out walking past some fast-foods or a baker's. This is usually where most people fail. Luckily, as long as you follow the tips, you will be able to overcome those obstacles and keep iron self-discipline.

Breakfasts - Instead of traditional toasts, traditional pancakes, waffles, and everything flour-based, go for the following swaps: eggs, sausages, bacon or ham, cheese, feta cheese, and some full-fat yogurt.

Salads - I recommend green chicken or avocado salad. You can ask the waiter to serve the dressing apart; they often contain sugar. If it's olive oil, you're good to go.

Burgers - if you're anything like me, going out almost always means burgers. Here comes the good news. You can eat them, however, with one caveat. The buns should be in a low-carb keto version. Alternatively, you can go for lettuce leaves to wrap the burger in. The most common trap to fall into is ketchup. It's usually loaded with refined sugar. Instead, use mayonnaise, mustard, sriracha, or any alternative sauce that's low on carbs.

Restaurants - who doesn't love Italian restaurants? Unfortunately, pasta or pizzas are a no-go. Opt for meat dishes and salads instead. At the Mexican, skip tortilla and burrito wraps (they are made from corn or flour). The same goes for rice and beans. The safest bet will be to order something with guacamole and/or sour cream, broccoli, green beans, asparagus, or other low-carb veggies.

Drinks - Stick to water, coffee, or tea with no sugar. No sodas, juices, or otherwise sweetened beverages. When it comes to alcohol, you can drink most of them pure - vodka, whiskey, rum, tequila, or gins – they are ok as they don't contain carbohydrates.

POULTRY

Cheese & Spinach Stuffed Chicken

SERVES: 4 | **PREPARATION TIME**: 50 MINUTES

Ingredients

4 chicken breasts, boneless and skinless

½ cup mozzarella cheese

1 ½ cups Parmesan cheese, shredded

6 ounces cream cheese

2 cups spinach, chopped

A pinch of nutmeg

½ tsp garlic, minced

Breading

2 eggs, beaten

1/3 cup almond flour

2 tbsp olive oil

½ tsp parsley

1/3 cup Parmesan cheese

A pinch of onion powder

Directions

1. Pound the chicken until it doubles in size. Mix cream cheese, spinach, mozzarella cheese, nutmeg, salt, pepper, and Parmesan cheese in a bowl. Divide the mixture between the chicken breasts and spread it out evenly. Wrap the chicken in a plastic wrap. Refrigerate for 15 minutes.

2. Preheat the oven to 370 F.

3. Beat the eggs and set aside. Combine all of the other breading ingredients in a bowl. Dip the chicken in eggs first, then in the breading mixture.

4. Warm the olive oil in a pan over medium heat. Cook the chicken in the pan until browned, about 5-6 minutes. Place on a lined baking sheet, and bake for 20 minutes. Serve.

Per Serving Calories 491, Net Carbs 3.5g, Fat 36g, Protein 38g

Asian Chicken with Fresh Lime-Peanut Sauce

SERVES: 6 | **PREPARATION TIME**: 1 HOUR AND 30 MINUTES

Ingredients

1 tbsp wheat-free soy sauce

1 tbsp sugar-free fish sauce

1 tbsp lime juice

1 tsp coriander

1 tsp garlic, minced

1 tsp ginger, minced

1 tbsp olive oil

1 tbsp rice wine vinegar

1 tsp cayenne pepper

1 tbsp erythritol

6 chicken thighs

Sauce:

½ cup peanut butter

1 tsp garlic, minced

1 tbsp lime juice

2 tbsp water

1 tsp ginger, minced

1 tbsp jalapeño, chopped

2 tbsp rice wine vinegar

2 tbsp erythritol

1 tbsp fish sauce

Directions

1. Combine all of the chicken ingredients in a large Ziploc bag.
2. Seal the bag and shake to combine.
3. Refrigerate for about 1 hour.
4. Remove from the fridge about 15 minutes before cooking.
5. Preheat the grill to medium, and grill the chicken for about 7 minutes per side.
6. Meanwhile, whisk together all of the sauce ingredients in a mixing bowl.
7. Serve the chicken drizzled with peanut sauce.

Per Serving Calories 492, Net Carbs 3g, Fat 36g, Protein 35g

Bacon-Wrapped Chicken with Grilled Asparagus

SERVES: 4 | **PREPARATION TIME**: 50 MINUTES

Ingredients

2 tbsp fresh lemon juice

6 chicken breasts

8 bacon slices

1 tbsp olive oil

1 lb asparagus spears

3 tbsp olive oil

Salt and black pepper to taste

Manchego cheese for topping

Directions

1. Preheat the oven to 400 F.

2. Season chicken breasts with salt and black pepper, and wrap 2 bacon slices around each chicken breast. Arrange on a baking sheet that is lined with parchment paper, drizzle with oil, and bake for 25-30 minutes until bacon is brown and crispy.

3. Preheat the grill.

4. Brush the asparagus spears with olive oil and season with salt. Grill turning frequently until slightly charred, 5-10 minutes.

5. Remove to a plate and drizzle with lemon juice. Grate over Manchego cheese so that it melts a little on contact with the hot asparagus and forms a cheesy dressing.

Per Serving Calories 468, Net Carbs 2g, Fat 38g, Protein 26g

Spicy Cheese Chicken Soup

SERVES: 4 | **PREPARATION TIME**: 15 MINUTES

Ingredients

½ cup salsa enchilada verde

2 cups chicken, cooked and shredded

2 cups chicken or bone broth

1 cup cheddar cheese, shredded

4 ounces cream cheese

½ tsp chili powder

½ tsp cumin, ground

½ tsp fresh cilantro, chopped

Salt and black pepper to taste

Directions

1. Combine the cream cheese, salsa verde, and broth in a food processor.
2. Pulse until smooth. Transfer the mixture to a pot and place over medium heat.
3. Cook until hot, but do not bring to a boil.
4. Add chicken, chili powder, and cumin, and cook for about 3-5 minutes, or until it is heated through. Stir in Cheddar cheese. Season with salt and pepper to taste.
5. Serve hot in individual bowls sprinkled with fresh cilantro.

Per Serving Calories 346, Net Carbs 3g, Fat 23g, Protein 25g

Bok Choy Caesar Salad with Chicken

SERVES: 4 | **PREPARATION TIME**: 1 HOUR AND 20 MINUTES

Ingredients

Chicken

4 chicken thighs, boneless and skinless
¼ cup lemon juice

2 garlic cloves, minced
2 tbsp olive oil

Salad

½ cup caesar salad dressing, sugar-free
2 tbsp olive oil
12 bok choy leaves

3 Parmesan cheese crisps
Parmesan cheese, grated or garnishing

Directions

1. Combine the chicken ingredients in a Ziploc bag. Seal the bag, shake to combine, and refrigerate for 1 hour.
2. Preheat the grill to medium heat, and grill the chicken about 4 minutes per side.
3. Cut bok choy leaves lengthwise, and brush it with oil. Grill for about 3 minutes. Place on a serving platter. Top with the chicken, and drizzle the dressing over. Sprinkle with Parmesan cheese and finish with Parmesan crisps to serve.

Per Serving Calories 529, Net Carbs 5g, Fat 39g, Protein 33g

Chicken & Spinach Gratin

Ingredients

6 chicken breasts, skinless and boneless

1 tsp mixed spice seasoning

Pink salt and black pepper to season

2 loose cups baby spinach

3 tsp olive oil

4 oz cream cheese, cubed

1 ¼ cups mozzarella cheese, shredded

4 tbsp water

Directions

1. Preheat oven to 375 F.

2. Season chicken with spice mix, salt, and black pepper. Pat with your hands to have the seasoning stick on the chicken.

3. Put in the casserole dish and layer spinach over the chicken.

4. Mix the oil with cream cheese, mozzarella, salt, and black pepper and stir in water a tablespoon at a time.

5. Pour the mixture over the chicken and cover the pot with aluminum foil.

6. Bake for 20 minutes, remove foil and continue cooking for 15 minutes until a beautiful golden brown color is formed on top.

7. Take out and allow sitting for 5 minutes. Serve warm with braised asparagus.

Per Serving Calories 340, Net Carbs 1g, Fat 30.2g, Protein 15g

Chili Chicken Kabobs with Tahini Dressing

Ingredients

3 tbsp soy sauce

1 tbsp ginger-garlic paste

2 tbsp swerve brown sugar

2 tbsp olive oil

3 chicken breasts, cut into bite-sized cubes

½ cup tahini

½ tsp garlic powder

Salt and chili pepper to taste

Directions

1. In a bowl, whisk soy sauce, ginger-garlic paste, swerve brown sugar, chili pepper, and olive oil. Put the chicken in a zipper bag, pour the marinade over, seal, and shake for an even coat. Marinate in the fridge for 2 hours.
2. Preheat a grill to 400 F and thread the chicken on skewers. Cook for 10 minutes in total with three to four turnings to be golden brown. Plate them.
3. Mix the tahini, garlic powder, salt, and ¼ cup of warm water in a bowl. Serve the chicken skewers and tahini dressing with cauliflower fried rice.

Per Serving Calories 225, Net Carbs 2g, Fat 17.4g, Protein 15g

Chicken with Eggplant & Tomatoes

SERVES: 4 | PREPARATION TIME: 25 MINUTES

Ingredients

2 tbsp ghee
1 lb chicken thighs
Salt and black pepper to taste
2 cloves garlic, minced

1 (14 oz) can whole tomatoes
1 eggplant, diced
10 fresh basil leaves, chopped + extra to garnish

Directions

1. Melt ghee in a saucepan over medium heat, season the chicken with salt and black pepper, and fry for 4 minutes on each side until golden brown. Remove the chicken onto a plate.
2. Sauté the garlic in the ghee for 2 minutes, pour in the tomatoes, and cook covered for 8 minutes. Include the eggplant and basil. Cook for 4 minutes.
3. Season the sauce with salt and black pepper, stir and add the chicken. Coat with sauce and simmer for 3 minutes.
4. Serve chicken with sauce on a bed of squash pasta garnished with basil.

Per Serving Calories 468, Net Carbs 2g, Fat 39.5g, Protein 26g

Tasty Chicken with Brussel Sprouts

SERVES: 8 | **PREPARATION TIME**: 120 MINUTES

Ingredients

5 pounds whole chicken

1 bunch oregano

1 bunch thyme

1 tbsp marjoram

1 tbsp parsley

1 tbsp olive oil

2 pounds Brussel sprouts

1 lemon

4 tbsp butter

Directions

1. Preheat your oven to 450 F.
2. Stuff the chicken with oregano, thyme, and lemon.
3. Make sure the wings are tucked over and behind.
4. Roast for 15 minutes. Reduce the heat to 325 F , and cook for 40 minutes.
5. Spread the butter over the chicken and sprinkle parsley and marjoram.
6. Add the Brussel sprouts. Return to oven and bake for 40 more minutes.
7. Let sit for 10 minutes before carving.

Per Serving Calories 430, Net Carbs 5g, Fat 32g, Protein 30g

Weekend Chicken with Grapefruit & Lemon

SERVES: 4 | **PREPARATION TIME**: 30 MINUTES

Ingredients

1 cup omission IPA

A pinch of garlic powder

1 tsp grapefruit zest

3 tbsp lemon juice

½ tsp coriander, ground

1 tbsp fish sauce

2 tbsp butter

¼ tsp xanthan gum

3 tbsp swerve sweetener

20 chicken wing pieces

Salt and black pepper to taste

Directions

1. Combine lemon juice and zest, fish sauce, coriander, omission IPA, sweetener, and garlic powder in a saucepan.
2. Bring to a boil, cover, lower the heat, and let simmer for 10 minutes.
3. Stir in the butter and xanthan gum. Set aside. Season the wings with some salt and pepper.
4. Preheat the grill and cook for 5 minutes per side.
5. Serve topped with the sauce.

Per Serving Calories 365, Net Carbs 4g, Fat 25g, Protein 21g

Rosemary Chicken with Avocado Sauce

SERVES: 4 | PREPARATION TIME: 22 MINUTES

Ingredients

1 avocado pitted

½ cup mayonnaise

3 tbsp ghee

4 chicken breasts

Salt and black pepper to taste

1 cup rosemary, chopped

½ cup chicken broth

Directions

1. Spoon avocado, mayonnaise, and salt into a food processor and puree until a smooth sauce is derived. Adjust the taste with salt. Pour sauce into a jar and refrigerate.
2. Melt ghee in a large skillet, season chicken with salt and black pepper, and fry for 4 minutes on each side to a golden brown. Remove chicken to a plate.
3. Pour the broth in the same skillet and add the cilantro. Bring to simmer covered for 3 minutes and add the chicken. Cover, and cook on low heat for 5 minutes until the liquid has reduced and chicken is fragrant.
4. Dish chicken only into serving plates and spoon the mayo-avocado sauce over.
5. Serve warm with buttered green beans and baby carrots.

Per Serving Calories 398, Net Carbs 4g, Fat 32g, Protein 24g

Turkey Patties with Cucumber Salsa

Ingredients

2 spring onions, thinly sliced

1 pound turkey, ground

1 egg

2 garlic cloves, minced

1 tbsp herbs, chopped

1 small chili pepper, deseeded and diced

2 tbsp ghee

Cucumber Salsa:

1 tbsp apple cider vinegar

1 tbsp dill, chopped

1 garlic clove, minced

2 cucumbers, grated

1 cup sour cream

1 jalapeño pepper, minced

2 tbsp olive oil

Directions

1. Place all of the turkey ingredients, except the ghee, in a bowl. Mix to combine. Make patties out of the mixture.

2. Melt ghee in a skillet over medium heat. Cook the patties for 3 minutes per side.

3. Place all of the salsa ingredients in a bowl and mix to combine. Serve the patties topped with salsa.

Per Serving Calories 475, Net Carbs 5g, Fat 38g, Protein 26g

Crispy Chicken with Eggs & Cheddar Cheese

Ingredients

2 eggs

3 tbsp butter, melted

3 cups coarsely crushed cheddar cheese

½ cup pork rinds, crushed

1 lb (not breaded) chicken tenders

Pink salt to season

Directions

1. Preheat oven to 350 F and line a baking sheet with parchment paper.
2. Whisk the eggs with the butter in a bowl and mix the cheese and pork rinds in another bowl.
3. Season chicken with salt, dip in egg mixture, and coat generously in cheddar mixture. Place onto the baking sheet, cover with aluminum foil, and bake for 25 minutes. Remove foil and cook further for 12 minutes to a golden brown.
4. Serve chicken with sweet mustard dip and veggie fries.

Per Serving Calories 203, Net Carbs 3g, Fat 14g, Protein 12g

Spinach Hasselback Chicken

SERVES: 6 | **PREPARATION TIME**: 45 MINUTES

Ingredients

4 ounces cream cheese

3 ounces mozzarella slices

10 ounces spinach

1/3 cup mozzarella, shredded

1 tbsp olive oil

1/3 cup tomato basil sauce

3 whole chicken breasts

Directions

1. Preheat your oven to 400 F.
2. Combine the cream cheese, shredded mozzarella, and spinach in the microwave until the cheese melts.
3. Cut the chicken with the knife a couple of times horizontally.
4. Stuff with the filling. Brush the top with olive oil.
5. Place on a lined baking dish and in the oven. Bake for 25 minutes.
6. Pour the sauce over, and top with mozzarella cheese. Return to oven, and cook for 5 minutes.

Per Serving Calories 338, Net Carbs 2.5g, Fat 28g, Protein 37g

Creamy Skillet Mushroom Chicken

SERVES: 6 | **PREPARATION TIME**: 35 MINUTES

Ingredients

2 cups mushrooms, sliced

½ tsp onion powder

½ tsp garlic powder

¼ cup butter

½ cup water

1 tsp Dijon mustard

1 tbsp tarragon, chopped

4 chicken thighs

Salt and black pepper to taste

Directions

1. Season the thighs with salt, pepper, garlic, and onion powder.
2. Melt some of the butter in a skillet and cook the chicken until browned. Set aside.
3. Melt the remaining butter and cook the mushrooms for about 5 minutes.
4. Stir in Dijon Mustard and water.
5. Return the chicken to the skillet. Season to taste with season and pepper.
6. Reduce the heat and cover, and let simmer for 15 minutes.
7. Stir in tarragon and serve.

Per Serving Calories 447, Net Carbs 1g, Fat 37g, Protein 31g

Mozzarella and Tomato Turkey Balls

SERVES: 4 | **PREPARATION TIME**: 15 MINUTES

Ingredients

1 pound turkey, ground

2 tbsp sun-dried tomatoes, chopped

2 tbsp basil, chopped

½ tsp garlic powder

1 egg

½ tsp salt

¼ cup almond flour

2 tbsp olive oil

½ cup mozzarella, shredded

¼ tsp black pepper

Directions

1. Place everything except the oil in a bowl.
2. Mix with your hands until combined.
3. Form 16 meatballs out of the mixture.
4. Heat the olive oil in a skillet over medium heat.
5. Cook the meatballs for about 3 minutes per each side.
6. Serve as desired and enjoy!

Per Serving Calories 310, Net Carbs 2g, Fat 26g, Protein 22g

Creamy Chicken with Mushroom Sauce

SERVES: 4 | **PREPARATION TIME**: 40 MINUTES

Ingredients

1 tbsp ghee

4 chicken breasts, cut into 8 chunks each

Salt and black pepper to taste

1 packet white onion soup mix

15 baby Bella mushrooms, sliced

1 cup cooking cream

1 small bunch parsley, chopped + extra to garnish

Directions

1. Melt ghee in a saucepan over medium heat, season the chicken with salt and black pepper, and brown on all sides for 6 minutes in total. Put in a plate.
2. Add the onion soup, mix, and simmer for 3 minutes and add the mushrooms and chicken. Cover and simmer for another 20 minutes.
3. Stir in the cream and parsley, cook on low heat for 3 minutes, and adjust taste with salt and black pepper.
4. Ladle the chicken with creamy sauce and mushrooms over four beds of cauliflower mash. Garnish with parsley and serve.

Per Serving Calories 448, Net Carbs 2g, Fat 38.2g, Protein 22g

Chicken Wings with White Sauce

SERVES: 6 | **PREPARATION TIME**: 25 MINUTES

Ingredients

1 cup plain yogurt

1 tsp fresh lemon juice

½ cup melted butter

2 pounds chicken wings

Salt and black pepper to taste

½ cup hot sauce

¼ cup Parmesan cheese, grated

Directions

1. Mix yogurt, lemon juice, salt, and black pepper in a bowl. Let chill.
2. Preheat oven to 400 F and season wings with salt and pepper.
3. Line a baking sheet and grease lightly with cooking spray.
4. Bake for 20 minutes until golden brown.
5. Mix butter, hot sauce, and parmesan in a bowl. Toss chicken in the sauce to evenly coat and plate.
6. Serve with yogurt dipping sauce and celery strips.

Per Serving Calories 452, Net Carbs 4g, Fat 36.4g, Protein 24g

Turkey Soup with Buffalo Sauce

SERVES: 4 | **PREPARATION TIME**: 15 MINUTES

Ingredients

2 cups turkey, cooked and shredded

3 tbsp butter, melted

4 cups chicken broth

4 tbsp cilantro, chopped

1/3 cup buffalo sauce

4 ounces cream cheese

Salt and black pepper to taste

Directions

1. Blend butter, buffalo sauce, and cream cheese in a food processor until smooth.
2. Transfer to a pot, add the chicken broth and heat until hot, but do not bring to a boil.
3. Stir in turkey, and cook until heated through.
4. Serve garnished with cilantro.

Per Serving Calories 406, Net Carbs 5g, Fat 29.5g, Protein 26.5g

Mediterranean Chicken with Tomato Sauce

SERVES: 6 | **PREPARATION TIME**: 20 MINUTES

Ingredients

2 tbsp butter

6 chicken thighs

Salt and black pepper to taste

14 oz can tomato sauce

2 tsp Italian seasoning

½ cup heavy cream

1 cup Parmesan cheese, shredded + extra to garnish.

Directions

1. In a saucepan, melt the butter over medium heat, season the chicken with salt and black pepper, and cook for 5 minutes on each side to brown. Plate the chicken.
2. Pour the tomato sauce and Italian seasoning in the pan, and cook covered for 8 minutes. Adjust taste with salt and black pepper.
3. Stir in the heavy cream and Parmesan cheese.
4. Once the cheese has melted, return the chicken to the pot.
5. Simmer for 4 minutes, making sure to coat the chicken with the sauce while cooking.
6. Dish the chicken with sauce, garnish with more Parmesan cheese.
7. Serve with zoodles.

Per Serving Calories 456, Net Carbs 2g, Fat 38.2g, Protein 24g

Chicken Thighs with Mustard and Thyme

SERVES: 4 | **PREPARATION TIME**: 30 MINUTES

Ingredients

½ cup chicken stock

1 tbsp olive oil

½ cup onion, chopped

4 chicken thighs

¼ cup heavy cream

2 tbsp Dijon mustard

1 tsp thyme

1 tsp garlic powder

Directions

1. Heat the olive oil in a pan. Cook the chicken for about 4 minutes per side. Set aside in a plate.

2. Sauté the onions in the same pan for 3 minutes, add the stock, and simmer for 5 minutes. Stir in mustard and heavy cream, along with thyme and garlic powder.

3. Pour the sauce over the chicken and serve.

Per Serving Calories 528, Net Carbs 4g, Fat 42g, Protein 33g

Savory Grilled Chicken with Broccoli

SERVES: 6 | **PREPARATION TIME**: 20 MINUTES

Ingredients

3 tbsp smoked paprika

Salt and black pepper to taste

2 tsp garlic powder

1 tbsp olive oil

6 chicken breasts

1 head broccoli, broken into florets

Directions

1. Place broccoli florets onto the steamer basket over the boiling water, steam for approximately 8 minutes, or until crisp-tender. Set aside.

2. Grease grill grate with cooking spray, and preheat grill to 400 F.

3. Combine paprika, salt, black pepper, and garlic powder in a bowl.

4. Brush chicken with olive oil and sprinkle spice mixture over chicken. Massage with your hands.

5. Grill chicken for 7 minutes per side until cooked through and brown on the outside and place on serving plates.

6. Serve warm with steamed broccoli.

Per Serving Calories 422, Net Carbs 2g, Fat 35.3g, Protein 26g

Chicken Sausage and Mozzarella Omelet

Ingredients

2 eggs

6 basil leaves

2 ounces mozzarella cheese

1 tbsp butter

1 tbsp water

5-8 thin chicken sausage slices

5 thin tomato slices

Salt and black pepper to taste

Directions

1. Whisk the eggs along with the water, and some salt and pepper.

2. Melt the butter in a skillet, and cook the eggs for 30 seconds.

3. Spread the sausage slices over. Arrange the sliced tomato and mozzarella over the chorizo. Cook for about 3 minutes.

4. Cover the skillet and continue cooking for 3 more minutes until the omelet is completely set.

5. When it is ready, remove the pan from heat, run a spatula around the edges of the frittata and flip it onto a warm plate, folded side down.

6. Serve garnished with basil leaves and a green salad.

Per Serving Calories 451, Net Carbs 3g, Fat 36.5g, Protein 30g

Zucchini and Turkey Bolognese Pasta

Ingredients

2 cups mushrooms, sliced

2 tsp olive oil

1 pound turkey, ground

3 tbsp pesto sauce

1 cup onion, diced

2 cups zucchini, sliced

6 cups veggie pasta (spiralized)

Directions

1. Heat the oil in a skillet. Add turkey, and cook until browned. Transfer to a plate.
2. Add onions to the skillet, and cook until translucent, about 3 minutes. Add zucchini and mushrooms, and cook for 7 more minutes. Return the turkey to the skillet. Stir in the pesto sauce. Cover the pan, lower the heat, and simmer for 5 minutes.

Per Serving Calories 273, Net Carbs 3.8g Fat 16g, Protein 19g

Skillet Browned Chicken with Creamy Greens

Ingredients

1 pound chicken thighs

2 tbsp coconut oil

2 tbsp coconut flour

2 carp dark leafy greens

1 tsp oregano

1 cup heavy cream

1 cup chicken broth

2 tbsp butter, melted

Directions

1. Melt the coconut oil in a skillet and brown the chicken on all sides. Set aside.
2. Melt the butter and whisk in the coconut flour. Whisk in the cream, and bring to a boil. Stir in oregano. Add in greens and cook until wilted. Pour the broth over and cook for a minute. Add the thighs in the skillet, and cook for an additional minute.

Per Serving Calories 446, Net Carbs 2.6g, Fat 38g, Protein 18g

PORK

Weekend Spicy Burgers with Sweet Onion

SERVES: 6 | **PREPARATION TIME**: 20 MINUTES

Ingredients

2 lb ground pork
Pink salt and chili pepper to taste
3 tbsp olive oil
1 tbsp butter
1 white onion, sliced into rings
1 tbsp balsamic vinegar
3 drops liquid stevia
6 low carb burger buns, halved
2 firm tomatoes, sliced into rings

Directions

1. Combine the pork, salt and chili pepper in a bowl, and mold out 6 patties.

2. Heat the olive oil in a skillet over medium heat, and fry the patties for 4 to 5 minutes on each side until golden brown on the outside. Remove onto a plate, and sit for 3 minutes.

3. Meanwhile, melt butter in a skillet over medium heat, sauté the onions for 2 minutes to be soft, and stir in the balsamic vinegar and liquid stevia. Cook for 30 seconds stirring once, or twice until caramelized.

4. In each bun, place a patty, top with some onion rings and 2 tomato rings.

5. Serve the burgers with cheddar cheese dip.

Per Serving Calories 315, Net Carbs 6g, Fat 23g, Protein 16g

Pork Chops with Raspberry Sauce

Ingredients

1 tbsp olive oil + extra, for brushing

2 lb pork chops

Pink salt and black pepper to taste

2 cups raspberries

¼ cup water

1 ½ tbsp Italian herb mix

3 tbsp balsamic vinegar

2 tsp sugar-free Worcestershire sauce

Directions

For the Chops

1. Heat oil in a skillet over medium heat, season the pork with salt and black pepper and cook for 5 minutes on each side. Put in serving plates, and reserve the pork drippings.

For the Sauce

2. Mash the raspberries with a fork in a bowl until jam-like. Pour into a medium saucepan, add the water, and herb mix. Bring to boil on low heat for 4 minutes.

3. Stir in the pork drippings, vinegar, and Worcestershire sauce. Simmer for 1 minute and turn the heat off.

4. Dish the pork chops, spoon sauce over, and serve with braised rapini.

Per Serving Calories 413, Net Carbs 1.1g, Fat 32.5g, Protein 26.3g

Creamy Pork Chops with Thyme

SERVES: 6 | **PREPARATION TIME**: 25 MINUTES

Ingredients

7 strips bacon, chopped

6 pork chops

Pink salt and black pepper to taste

5 sprigs fresh thyme + extra to garnish

¼ cup chicken broth

½ cup heavy cream

Directions

1. Cook bacon in a large skillet over medium heat for 5 minutes to crispy. Remove with a slotted spoon onto a paper towel-lined plate to soak up excess fat.
2. Season pork chops with salt and black pepper, and brown in the bacon grease for 4 minutes on each side. Remove to the bacon plate.
3. Stir the thyme, chicken broth, and heavy cream in the same skillet, and simmer for 5 minutes. Season with salt and black pepper.
4. Put the chops and bacon in the skillet, and cook further for another 2 minutes.
5. Serve chops and a generous ladle of sauce with cauli mash. Garnish with thyme.

Per Serving Calories 435, Net Carbs 3g, Fat 37g, Protein 22g

Spicy Pork with Peanut Butter & Veggies

SERVES: 6 | **PREPARATION TIME**: 22 MINUTES

Ingredients

1 ½ tbsp ghee

2 lb pork loin, cut into strips

Pink salt and chili pepper to taste

2 tsp ginger-garlic paste

¼ cup chicken broth

5 tbsp peanut butter

2 cups mixed stir-fry vegetables

Directions

1. Melt the ghee in a wok and mix the pork with salt, chili pepper, and ginger-garlic paste. Cook for 6 minutes until no longer pink.
2. Mix the peanut butter with some broth to be smooth, add to the pork and stir; cook for 2 minutes.
3. Pour in the remaining broth, cook for 4 minutes, and add the mixed veggies. Simmer for 5 minutes.
4. Adjust the taste with salt and black pepper, and spoon the stir-fry to a side of cilantro cauliflower rice.

Per Serving Calories 371, Net Carbs 1g, Fat 29g, Protein 22.5g

Garlic Lemon Pork Chops with Brussel Sprouts

SERVES: 6 | **PREPARATION TIME**: 30 MINUTES

Ingredients

3 tbsp lemon juice

3 cloves garlic, pureed

Pink salt and black pepper to taste

1 tbsp olive oil

6 Pork loin chops

1 tbsp butter

1 lb Brussel sprouts, trimmed and halved

2 tbsp white wine

Kosher salt and black pepper to season

Directions

1. Preheat grill to 400 F, and mix the lemon juice, garlic, salt, pepper, and oil in a bowl.
2. Brush the pork with mixture, place into a baking sheet, and cook for 6 minutes on each side until browned.
3. Share into 6 plates, and make the side dish.
4. Melt butter in a small wok, or pan and cook in Brussel sprouts for 5 minutes until tender. Drizzle with white wine, sprinkle with salt and black pepper, and cook for another 5 minutes.
5. Ladle Brussel sprouts to the side of the chops, and serve with a hot sauce.

Per Serving Calories 549, Net Carbs 2g, Fat 48g, Protein 26g

Ricotta with Squash and Sausage Omelet

SERVES: 1 | **PREPARATION TIME**: 10 MINUTES

Ingredients

2 eggs

1 cup kale, chopped

4 oz sausages, chopped

2 tbsp ricotta cheese

4 oz squash, roasted

1 tbsp olive oil

Salt and black pepper to taste

Fresh parsley to garnish

Directions

1. Beat the eggs in a bowl, season with salt and pepper, and stir with the kale and the ricotta.
2. In another bowl, mash the squash.
3. Add the squash to the egg mixture.
4. Heat ¼ tbsp. of olive oil in a pan over medium heat.
5. Add sausage, and cook until browned on all sides, turning occasionally.
6. Drizzle the remaining olive oil. Pour the egg mixture over.
7. Cook for about 2 minutes per side until the eggs are thoroughly cooked, and lightly browned.
8. Remove the pan, and run a spatula around the edges of the omelet, slide it onto a warm platter. Fold in half, and serve sprinkled with fresh parsley.

Per Serving Calories 258, Net Carbs 3.5g, Fat 21.7g, Protein 12.3g

Baked Pulled Pork Nachos

SERVES: 4 | **PREPARATION TIME**: 15 MINUTES

Ingredients

1 bag (13 oz) almond flour tortilla chips
2 cups leftover pulled pork
1 red bell pepper, seeded and chopped

1 red onion, diced
2 cups Monterey Jack cheese, shredded

Directions

1. Preheat oven to 350 F.
2. Arrange the chips in a medium cast iron pan, scatter pork over, followed by red bell pepper, onion, and sprinkle with cheese.
3. Place the pan in the oven, and cook for 10 minutes until the cheese has melted.
4. Allow cooling for 3 minutes and serve.

Per Serving Calories 352, Net Carbs 9.3g, Fat 25g, Protein 22g

Easy Chorizo Soup with Cauliflower & Turnip

SERVES: 4 | **PREPARATION TIME**: 40 MINUTES

Ingredients

1 cauliflower head, chopped

1 turnip, chopped

3 tbsp butter

1 chorizo sausage, sliced

2 cups chicken broth

1 small onion, chopped

2 cups water

Salt and black pepper to taste

Directions

1. Melt 2 tbsp. of the butter in a large pot over medium heat.
2. Stir in onions and cook until soft and golden, about 6 minutes.
3. Add cauliflower and turnip, and cook for another 5 minutes.
4. Pour the broth and water over. Bring to a boil, simmer covered, and cook for about 20 minutes until the vegetables are tender. Remove from heat.
5. Melt the remaining butter in a skillet.
6. Add the chorizo and cook for 5 minutes until crispy.
7. Blitz the soup with a hand blender until smooth. Taste and adjust the seasonings.
8. Serve the soup in deep bowls topped with the chorizo.

Per Serving Calories 251, Net Carbs 5.7g, Fat 19g, Protein 10g

BBQ Grilled Ribs

SERVES: 4 | **PREPARATION TIME**: 50 MINUTES

Ingredients

2 tbsp xylitol

Salt and black pepper to taste

1 tbsp olive oil

3 tsp chipotle powder

1 tsp garlic powder

1 lb pork spare ribs

4 tbsp sugar-free BBQ sauce + extra for serving

Directions

1. Mix the monk fruit syrup, salt, pepper, oil, chipotle, and garlic powder. Brush on the meaty sides of the ribs, and wrap in foil. Sit for 30 minutes to marinate.
2. Preheat oven to 400 F, place wrapped ribs on a baking sheet, and cook for 40 minutes to be cooked through.
3. Remove ribs and aluminum foil, brush with BBQ sauce, and brown under the broiler for 10 minutes on both sides.
4. Slice and serve with extra BBQ sauce and lettuce tomato salad.

Per Serving Calories 395, Net Carbs 3g, Fat 33g, Protein 21g

Spicy Pork Lettuce Wraps

SERVES: 6 | **PREPARATION TIME**: 20 MINUTES

Ingredients

2 lb ground pork

1 tbsp ginger-garlic paste

Pink salt and chili pepper to taste

1 tsp ghee

1 fresh head iceberg lettuce

2 sprigs green onion, chopped

1 red bell pepper, seeded and chopped

½ cucumber, finely chopped

Directions

1. Put the pork with ginger-garlic, salt, and chili pepper seasoning in a saucepan. Cook for 10 minutes over medium heat while breaking any lumps until the beef is no longer pink.
2. Drain liquid and add the ghee, melt, and brown the meat for 4 minutes with continuous stirring. Turn the heat off.
3. Pat the lettuce dry with paper towel and in each leaf spoon two to three tablespoons of pork, top with green onions, bell pepper, and cucumber.
4. Serve with soy drizzling sauce.

Per Serving Calories 311, Net Carbs 1g, Fat 24.3g, Protein 19g

Tart with Meat and Mashed Cauliflower

SERVES: 8 | **PREPARATION TIME**: 1 HOUR AND 40 MINUTES

Ingredients

Crust:

1 egg
¼ cup butter
2 cups almond flour
¼ tsp xanthan gum
¼ cup mozzarella, shredded
A pinch of salt

Filling:

2 pounds ground pork
1/3 cup onion, pureed
¾ tsp allspice
1 cup cauliflower, cooked and mashed
1 tbsp ground sage
2 tbsp butter

Directions

1. Preheat your oven to 350 F.
2. Whisk together all of the crust ingredients in a bowl. Make two balls out of the mixture, and refrigerate for 10 minutes.
3. Melt the butter in a pan over medium heat and add the ground pork. Cook for about 10 minutes, stirring occasionally. Remove to a bowl. Add in the other ingredients and mix to combine.
4. Roll out the tart crusts and place one at the bottom of a greased baking pan. Spread the filling over the crust. Top with the other coat.
5. Bake for 50 minutes, then serve.

Per Serving Calories 485, Net Carbs 4g, Fat 41g, Protein 29g

Butternut Squash & Pork Stew

Ingredients

1 cup butternut squash

2 pounds pork, chopped

1 tbsp peanut butter

4 tbsp peanuts, chopped

1 garlic clove, minced

½ cup onion, chopped

½ cup white wine

1 tbsp olive oil

1 tsp lemon juice

¼ cup sweetener, granulated

¼ tsp cardamom

¼ tsp all spice

2 cups chicken stock

Directions

1. Heat the olive oil in a large pot. Add onions and sauté for 3 minutes until translucent. Add garlic, and cook for 30 more seconds.

2. Add the pork, and cook until browned, about 5-6 minutes, stirring periodically. Pour in the wine, and cook for one minute.

3. Throw in the remaining ingredients, except for the lemon juice and peanuts.

4. Add two cups of water, bring the mixture to a boil, and cook for 5 minutes.

5. Reduce the heat to low, cover the pot, and let cook for about 30 minutes. Adjust seasoning.

6. Stir in the lemon juice before serving.

7. Ladle into serving bowls, and serve topped with peanuts, and enjoy.

Per Serving Calories 451, Net Carbs 4g, Fat 33g, Protein 27.5g

BEEF AND LAMB

Cotija Beef Burgers

SERVES: 3 | **PREPARATION TIME**: 14 MINUTES

Ingredients

1 lb ground beef

1 tsp parsley, dried

½ tsp sugar-free Worcestershire sauce

Salt and black pepper to taste

1 cup cotija cheese, shredded

4 almond flour buns, halved

Directions

1. Preheat a grill to 400 F, and grease the grate with cooking spray.
2. Mix the beef, parsley, Worcestershire sauce, salt, and black pepper with your hands until evenly combined. Make medium sized patties out of the mixture, about 4 patties.
3. Cook on the grill for 7 minutes one side to be cooked through and no longer pink.
4. Flip the patties and top with cheese. Cook for another 7 minutes to be well done while the cheese melts onto the meat.
5. Remove the patties, and sandwich into two halves of a bun each.
6. Serve with a tomato dipping sauce and zucchini fries.

Per Serving Calories 386, Net Carbs 2g, Fat 32g, Protein 21g

Flank Steak Pinwheels

SERVES: 6 | **PREPARATION TIME**: 40 MINUTES

Ingredients

1 ½ lb beef flank steak

Pink salt and black pepper to season

2/3 cup feta cheese, crumbled

½ loose cup baby spinach

1 jalapeño pepper, chopped

¼ cup basil leaves, chopped

Directions

1. Preheat oven to 400 F, and grease a baking sheet with cooking spray.
2. Wrap the steak in plastic wrap, place on a flat surface, and gently run a rolling pin over to flatten. Take off the wraps.
3. Sprinkle with half of the feta cheese, top with spinach, jalapeno, basil leaves, and the remaining cheese.
4. Carefully roll the steak over on the stuffing and secure with toothpicks.
5. Place in the greased baking sheet, and cook for 15 minutes, flipping once until nicely browned on the outside and the cheese melted within.
6. Cool for 3 minutes, slice into pinwheels, and serve with thyme sautéed veggies.

Per Serving Calories 490, Net Carbs 2g, Fat 41g, Protein 28g

Rack of Lamb with Lemony Sauce

SERVES: 4 | **PREPARATION TIME**: 25 MINUTES

Ingredients

8 lamb rack

2 tbsp favorite spice mix

1 tsp olive oil

Sauce:

¼ cup olive oil

1 tsp red pepper flakes

2 tbsp lemon juice

2 tbsp fresh mint

3 garlic cloves, pressed

2 tbsp lemon zest

¼ cup parsley

½ tsp smoked paprika

Directions

1. Rub the lamb with the oil and sprinkle with the seasoning.
2. Preheat the grill to medium. Grill the lamb racks for about 3 minutes per side.
3. Whisk together the sauce ingredients. Serve the lamb with the sauce.

Per Serving Calories 392, Net Carbs 0g, Fat 31g, Protein 29g

Creamy Reuben Soup

Ingredients

1 onion, diced

7 cups beef stock

1 tsp caraway seeds

2 celery stalks, diced

2 garlic cloves, minced

¾ tsp black pepper

2 cups heavy cream

1 cup sauerkraut

1 pound corned beef, chopped

3 tbsp butter

1 ½ cups Swiss cheese

Salt and black pepper to taste

Directions

1. Melt the butter in a large pot. Add onions and celery, and fry for 3 minutes until tender. Add garlic, and cook for another minute.
2. Pour the broth over and stir in sauerkraut, salt, caraway seeds, and add a pinch of pepper.
3. Bring to a boil. Reduce the heat to low, and add the corned beef.
4. Cook for about 15 minutes. Adjust the seasoning.
5. Stir in heavy cream and cheese, and cook for 1 minute.

Per Serving Calories 450, Net Carbs 8g, Fat 37g, Protein 23g

Lamb Chops with Sage & White Wine

Ingredients

6 lamb chops

1 tbsp sage

1 tsp thyme

1 onion, sliced

1 cup water

3 garlic cloves, minced

2 tbsp olive oil

½ cup white wine

Salt and black pepper to taste

Directions

1. Heat the olive oil in a pan. Add onions and garlic, and cook for a few minutes, until soft. Rub the sage and thyme over the lamb chops.
2. Cook the lamb for about 3 minutes per side. Set aside.
3. Pour the white wine and water into the pan, bring the mixture to a boil.
4. Cook until the liquid is reduced by half. Add the chops in the pan, reduce the heat, and let simmer for 1 hour.

Per Serving Calories 397, Net Carbs 4.3g, Fat 30g, Protein 16g

Slow Cooked Sausage and Cheddar Beer Soup

SERVES: 8 | **PREPARATION TIME:** 8 HOURS

Ingredients

1 cup heavy cream

10 ounces beef sausages, sliced

1 cup celery, chopped

1 cup carrots, chopped

4 garlic cloves, minced

8 ounces cream cheese

1 tsp red pepper flakes

6 ounces beer

16 ounces beef stock

1 onion, diced

1 cups cheddar cheese

Salt and black pepper to taste

Fresh cilantro, chopped, to garnish

Directions

1. Heat the slow cooker on Low.
2. Add broth, beer, sausage, carrots, onion, celery, salt, red pepper flakes, salt, and pepper, and stir to combine. Add enough water to cover all the ingredients by roughly 2 inches. Close the lid and cook for 6 hours.
3. Open the lid and stir in the heavy cream, cheddar, and cream cheese, and cook for 2 more hours.
4. Ladle the soup into bowls, and garnish with cilantro before serving.

Per Serving Calories 244, Net Carbs 4g, Fat 17g, Protein 5g

Zucchini Stuffed with Beef, Onion & Cheese

SERVES: 4 | **PREPARATION TIME**: 25 MINUTES

Ingredients

4 zucchinis

2 tbsp olive oil

1 ½ lb ground beef

1 medium red onion, chopped

2 tbsp pimiento rojo, chopped

Pink salt and black pepper to taste

1 cup yellow cheddar cheese, grated

Directions

1. Preheat oven to 350 F.
2. Lay the zucchinis on a flat surface, trim off the ends, and cut in half lengthwise. Scoop out pulp from each half with a spoon to make shells. Chop the flesh.
3. Heat oil in a skillet; add the ground beef, red onion, pimiento, and zucchini pulp, and season with salt and black pepper. Cook for 6 minutes while stirring to break up lumps until beef is no longer pink. Turn the heat off.
4. Spoon the beef into the boats, and sprinkle with cheddar cheese.
5. Place on a greased baking sheet, and cook to melt the cheese for 15 minutes until zucchini boats are tender.
6. Take out, cool for 2 minutes, and serve warm with a mixed green salad.

Per Serving Calories 335, Net Carbs 7g, Fat 24g, Protein 18g

Cauli Rice with Vegetables and Beef Steak

SERVES: 4 | **PREPARATION TIME**: 25 MINUTES

Ingredients

2 cups cauli rice

3 cups mixed vegetables

3 tbsp ghee

1 lb beef skirt steak

Salt and black pepper to taste

4 fresh eggs

Hot sauce (sugar-free) for topping

Directions

1. Mix the cauliflower rice with mixed vegetables in a bowl, sprinkle with a little water, and steam in the microwave for 1 minute to tender. Share into 4 serving bowls.

2. Melt the ghee in a skillet, season the beef with salt and pepper, and brown in the ghee for 5 minutes on each side. Use a perforated spoon to ladle the meat onto the vegetables.

3. Wipe out the skillet and return to medium heat, crack in an egg, season with salt and pepper, and cook until the egg white has set, but the yolk is still runny 3 minutes.

4. Remove egg onto the vegetable bowl, and fry the remaining 3 eggs. Add to the other bowls.

5. Drizzle the beef bowl with hot sauce, and serve.

Per Serving Calories 320, Net Carbs 4g, Fat 26g, Protein 15g

Bunless Beef Burgers with Sriracha

SERVES: 4 | **PREPARATION TIME**: 15 MINUTES

Ingredients

1 pound ground beef
½ tsp onion powder
½ tsp garlic powder
2 tbsp ghee
1 tsp Dijon mustard

4 keto buns
¼ cup mayonnaise
1 tsp sriracha
4 tbsp cole slaw

Directions

1. Mix together beef, onion, garlic powder, mustard, salt and pepper. Create 4 burgers.

2. Melt the ghee in a skillet, and cook the burgers for about 3 minutes per side.

3. Serve on a bun topped with mayonnaise, sriracha and slaw.

Per Serving Calories 664, Net Carbs 7.9g, Fat 55g, Protein 39g

Cheese Beef Burgers with Cauli Rice Casserole

Ingredients

2 lb ground beef

Pink salt and black pepper to taste

1 cup cauli rice

2 cups cabbage, chopped

14 oz can diced tomatoes

1/4 cup water

1 cup Colby Jack cheese, shredded

Directions

1. Preheat oven to 375 F, and grease a baking dish with cooking spray.

2. Put beef in a pot and season with salt and black pepper, and cook over medium heat for 6 minutes until no longer pink. Drain grease.

3. Add cauliflower rice, cabbage, tomatoes, and water. Stir and bring to boil covered for 5 minutes to thicken the sauce. Adjust taste with salt and black pepper.

4. Spoon the beef mixture into the baking dish, and spread evenly in the dish. Sprinkle with cheese, and bake in the oven for 15 minutes until cheese has melted and golden brown. Remove, cool for 4 minutes, and serve.

Per Serving Calories 335, Net Carbs 5g, Fat 25g, Protein 20g

Grandma's Meatloaf with Balsamic Glaze

Ingredients

3 pounds ground beef

½ cup onion, chopped

½ cup almond flour

2 garlic cloves, minced

1 cup mushrooms, sliced

3 eggs

Salt and black pepper to taste

2 tbsp parsley, chopped

¼ cup bell peppers, chopped

1/3 cup Parmesan cheese, grated

1 tsp balsamic vinegar

Glaze:

2 cups balsamic vinegar

1 tbsp sweetener

2 tbsp sugar-free ketchup

Directions

1. Combine all of the meatloaf ingredients in a large bowl. Press the mixture into greased loaf pan. Bake at 375 F for about 30 minutes.

2. Meanwhile, make the glaze by combining all of the ingredients in a saucepan over medium heat. Simmer for 20 minutes, until the glaze is thickened.

3. Pour ¼ cup of the glaze over the meatloaf. Save the extra for future use. Put the meatloaf back in the oven, and cook for 20 more minutes.

Per Serving Calories 264, Net Carbs 6g, Fat 19g, Protein 23g

Creole Beef Tripe Stew

SERVES: 6 | **PREPARATION TIME**: 30 MINUTES + 3 HOURS REFRIGERATION

Ingredients

1 ½ lb beef tripe

4 cups buttermilk

Pink salt to taste

2 tsp Creole seasoning

3 tbsp olive oil

2 large onions, sliced

3 tomatoes, diced

Directions

1. Put tripe in a bowl, and cover with buttermilk. Refrigerate for 3 hours to extract bitterness and gamey taste. Remove from buttermilk, pat dry with paper towels, and season with salt and creole seasoning.

2. Heat 2 tablespoons of oil in a skillet over medium heat and brown the tripe on both sides for 6 minutes in total. Remove, and set aside. Add the remaining oil, and sauté onions for 3 minutes. Include the tomatoes and cook for 10 minutes. Put the tripe in the sauce, and cook for 3 minutes. Serve with cauli rice.

Per Serving Calories 342, Net Carbs 1g, Fat 27g, Protein 22g

Cauliflower Curry with Ground Beef

SERVES: 6 | **PREPARATION TIME**: 25 MINUTES

Ingredients

1 tbsp olive oil

1 ½ lb ground beef

1 tbsp ginger-garlic paste

1 tsp garam masala

1 (7 oz) can whole tomatoes

1 small head cauliflower, cut into florets

Pink salt and chili pepper to taste

¼ cup water

Directions

1. Heat oil in a saucepan over medium heat, add the beef, ginger-garlic paste and season with garam masala.
2. Cook for 5 minutes while breaking any lumps.
3. Stir in the tomatoes and cauliflower, season with salt and chili pepper, and cook covered for 6 minutes.
4. Add the water and bring to a boil over medium heat for 10 minutes, or until the liquid has reduced by half. Adjust taste with salt.
5. Serve with shirataki rice.

Per Serving Calories 374, Net Carbs 2g, Fat 33g, Protein 22g

FISH AND SEAFOOD

Salmon Crusted with Pistachio Nuts and Sauce

SERVES: 4 | **PREPARATION TIME**: 35 MINUTES

Ingredients

4 salmon fillets
½ tsp pepper
1 tsp salt
¼ cup mayonnaise
½ cup pistachios, chopped

Sauce

1 shallot, chopped
2 tsp lemon zest
1 tbsp olive oil
A pinch of pepper
1 cup heavy cream

Directions

1. Preheat the oven to 375 F.
2. Brush the salmon with mayonnaise and season with salt and pepper.
3. Coat with pistachios
4. Place in a lined baking dish, and bake, for 15 minutes.
5. Meanwhile, heat the olive oil in a saucepan, and sauté the shallots, for a few minutes. Stir in the rest of the sauce ingredients.
6. Bring the mixture to a boil, and cook until thickened.
7. Serve the salmon topped with the sauce.

Per Serving Calories 563, Net Carbs 6g, Fat 47g, Protein 34g

Greek Tilapia with Herbs

SERVES: 4 | **PREPARATION TIME**: 30 MINUTES

Ingredients

4 tilapia fillets

2 garlic cloves, minced

2 tsp oregano

14 ounces tomatoes, diced

1 tbsp olive oil

½ red onion, chopped

2 tbsp parsley

¼ cup kalamata olives

Directions

1. Heat the olive oil in a skillet over medium heat, and cook the onion, for about 3 minutes. Add garlic and oregano, and cook, for 30 seconds.
2. Stir in tomatoes and bring the mixture to a boil.
3. Reduce the heat and simmer, for 5 minutes.
4. Add olives and tilapia.
5. Cook, for about 8 minutes.
6. Serve the tilapia with the tomato sauce. Enjoy!

Per Serving Calories 182, Net Carbs 6g, Fat 15g, Protein 23g

Cilantro Shrimp Stew with Sriracha Sauce

SERVES: 6 | **PREPARATION TIME**: 25 MINUTES

Ingredients

1 cup coconut milk

2 tbsp lime juice

¼ cup diced roasted peppers

1 ½ pounds shrimp, peeled and deveined

¼ cup olive oil

1 garlic clove, minced

14 ounces diced tomatoes

2 tbsp sriracha sauce

¼ cup onions, chopped

¼ cup cilantro, chopped

Fresh dill, chopped to garnish

Salt and black pepper to taste

Directions

1. Heat the olive oil in a pot over medium heat.
2. Add onions and, cook for 3 minutes, or until translucent.
3. Add the garlic and cook, for another minute, until soft. Add tomatoes, shrimp, and cilantro.
4. Cook until the shrimp becomes opaque, about 3-4 minutes.
5. Stir in sriracha and coconut milk, and cook, for 2 more minutes. Do NOT bring to a boil. Stir in the lime juice, and season with salt and pepper to taste.
6. Spoon the stew in bowls, garnish with fresh dill, and serve warm.

Per Serving Calories 324, Net Carbs 5g, Fat 21g, Protein 23g

Salmon Omelet with Avocado

SERVES: 1 | **PREPARATION TIME**: 15 MINUTES

Ingredients

½ avocado, sliced

2 tbsp chives, chopped

2 oz smoked salmon, cut into strips

1 spring onion, sliced

3 eggs

2 tbsp cream cheese

1 tbsp butter

Salt and black pepper to taste

Directions

1. In a small bowl, combine the chives and cream cheese. Set aside.
2. Now, beat the eggs in a large bowl and season with salt and pepper.
3. Melt the butter in a pan over medium heat.
4. Add the eggs to the pan and cook, for about 3 minutes.
5. Carefully flip the omelet over and continue cooking for 2 minutes until golden.
6. Remove the omelet to a plate and spread the chive mixture over.
7. Arrange the salmon, avocado, and onion slices. Wrap the omelet. Serve immediately.

Per Serving Calories 514, Net Carbs 5.8g, Fat 48g, Protein 37g

Green Bean Mackerel Salad

Ingredients

2 mackerel fillets

2 hardboiled eggs, sliced

1 tbsp coconut oil

2 cups green beans

1 avocado, sliced

4 cups mixed salad greens

2 tbsp olive oil

2 tbsp lemon juice

1 tsp Dijon mustard

Salt and black pepper to taste

Directions

1. Fill a saucepan with water and add the beans and some salt.
2. Cook over medium heat for about 3 minutes. Drain and set aside.
3. Melt the coconut oil in a pan over medium heat. Add the mackerel fillets, and cook, for about 4 minutes per side or until opaque and crispy.
4. Divide greens between salad bowls. Top with mackerel, egg, and avocado slices.
5. In a separate bowl, whisk together the lemon juice, olive oil, mustard, salt, and pepper, and drizzle over the salad.

Per Serving Calories 525, Net Carbs 7.6g, Fat 42g, Protein 27.3g

Salmon with Herby Cream Sauce

Ingredients

2 salmon fillets

¾ tsp tarragon

1 tbsp duck fat

¾ tsp dill

Sauce

2 tbsp butter

½ tsp dill

½ tsp tarragon

¼ cup heavy cream

Directions

1. Season the salmon with dill and tarragon.
2. Melt the duck fat in a pan over medium heat.
3. Add salmon, and cook, for about 4 minutes on both sides. Set aside.
4. Melt the butter and add the dill and tarragon.
5. Cook, for 30 seconds to infuse the flavors.
6. Whisk in the heavy cream, and cook, for one more minute.
7. Serve the salmon topped with the sauce.

Per Serving Calories 468, Net Carbs 1.5g, Fat 40g, Protein 22g

Spicy Blackened Tilapia Tacos with Cabbage Slaw

SERVES: 4 | **PREPARATION TIME**: 20 MINUTES

Ingredients

1 tbsp olive oil

1 tsp chili powder

2 tilapia fillets

1 tsp paprika

4 keto tortillas

Slaw:

½ cup red cabbage, shredded

1 tbsp lemon juice

1 tsp apple cider vinegar

1 tbsp olive oil

Directions

1. Season the tilapia with chili powder and paprika.
2. Heat the olive oil in a skillet over medium heat.
3. Add tilapia, and cook until blackened, about 3 minutes per side.
4. Cut into strips.
5. Divide the tilapia between the tortillas.
6. Combine all of the slaw ingredients in a bowl. Divide the slaw between the tortillas.

Per Serving Calories 260, Net Carbs 3.5g, Fat 20g, Protein 13.8g

Saucy Butter Shrimp

SERVES: 2 | **PREPARATION TIME**: 30 MINUTES

Ingredients

½ ounce Parmesan cheese, grated

1 tbsp water

1 egg, beaten

¼ tsp curry powder

2 tsp almond flour

12 shrimp, shelled

3 tbsp coconut oil

Sauce

2 tbsp curry leaves

2 tbsp butter

½ onion, diced

½ cup heavy cream

½ ounce cheddar

Directions

1. Combine all of the dry ingredients for the batter.
2. Melt the coconut oil in a skillet over medium heat. Dip the shrimp in the egg first, and then coat with the dry mixture.
3. Fry until golden and crispy. In another skillet, melt the butter. Add onions, and cook, for 3 minutes. Add curry leaves, and cook for 30 seconds.
4. Stir in heavy cream and cheddar and cook until thickened. Add the shrimp and coat them well. Serve.

Per Serving Calories 560, Net Carbs 4.3g, Fat 56g, Protein 18.4g

Easy Shrimp with Red Wine Sauce

SERVES: 4 | **PREPARATION TIME**: 45 MINUTES

Ingredients

1 pound shrimp, peeled and deveined

2 tbsp olive oil

Juice of 1 lime

Red wine sauce:

½ tsp salt

¼ cup olive oil

2 garlic cloves

¼ cup red onion, chopped

¼ cup red wine vinegar

½ tsp pepper

2 cups parsley

¼ tsp red pepper flakes

Directions

1. Place the sauce ingredients in the blender. Process until smooth. Set aside.
2. Combine shrimp, olive oil and lime juice in a bowl, and let marinate in the fridge, for 30 minutes.
3. Preheat your grill to medium. Add shrimp, and cook about 2 minutes per side.
4. Serve shrimp drizzled with the sauce.

Per Serving Calories 283, Net Carbs 3.5g, Fat 20.3g, Protein 16g

Lemon Crab Cakes

SERVES: 8 | **PREPARATION TIME**: 15 MINUTES

Ingredients

2 tbsp coconut oil

1 tbsp lemon juice

1 cup lump crab meat

2 tbsp parsley

2 tsp Dijon mustard

1 egg, beaten

1 ½ tbsp coconut flour

Directions

1. Check to make sure that there are no shells left in the crab meat and place it in a bowl. Add the remaining ingredients, except coconut oil.
2. Mix well to combine. Make 8 crab cakes out of the mixture.
3. Melt the coconut oil in a skillet over medium heat.
4. Add the crab cakes, and cook for about 2-3 minutes per side.

Per Serving Calories 65, Net Carbs 3.6g, Fat 5g, Protein 5.3g

Tuna Salad with Lime Mayo

SERVES: 2 | **PREPARATION TIME**: 5 MINUTES

Ingredients

1 cup canned tuna, drained

1 tsp onion flakes

3 tbsp mayonnaise

1 cup romaine lettuce, shredded

1 tbsp lime juice

Sea salt to taste

6 black olives, pitted and sliced

Directions

1. Combine tuna, mayonnaise, lime juice, and salt to taste in a bowl and mix.

2. In a salad platter, arrange the shredded lettuce and onion flakes. Spread the tuna mixture over; top with black olives, and serve well-chilled.

Per Serving Calories 248, Net Carbs 2g, Fat 20g, Protein 18.5g

Zucchini Noodles with Sardines & Capers

SERVES: 2 | **PREPARATION TIME**: 10 MINUTES

Ingredients

4 cups zoodles

2 ounces cubed bacon

4 ounces canned sardines, chopped

½ cup canned tomatoes, chopped

1 tbsp capers

1 tbsp parsley

1 tsp garlic, minced

Directions

1. Pour some of the sardine oil in a pan. Add garlic, and cook, for 1 minute.

2. Add the bacon, and cook, for 2 more minutes. Stir in the tomatoes, and let simmer, for 5 minutes. Add zoodles and sardines, and cook, for 3 minutes.

Per Serving Calories 230, Net Carbs 6g, Fat 31g, Protein 20g

Homemade Lobster Salad Rolls

SERVES: 4 | **PREPARATION TIME**: 1 HOUR 10 MINUTES

Ingredients

5 cups cauliflower florets

1/3 cup celery, diced

2 cups large shrimp, cooked

1 tbsp bill, chopped

½ cup mayonnaise

1 tsp apple cider vinegar

¼ tsp celery seeds

2 tbsp lemon juice

2 tsp swerve sweetener

Salt and black pepper to taste

Directions

1. Combine cauliflower, celery, shrimp, and dill in a large bowl.

2. Whisk mayonnaise, vinegar, celery seeds, sweetener, and lemon juice in another bowl. Season with salt. Pour the dressing over the salad, and gently toss to combine. Serve cold.

Per Serving Calories 182, Net Carbs 2g, Fat 15g, Protein 12g

Sea Bass with Hazelnuts

SERVES: 2 | **PREPARATION TIME**: 30 MINUTES

Ingredients

2 sea bass fillets

2 tbsp butter, melted

1/3 cup hazelnuts, roasted

A pinch of cayenne pepper

Directions

1. Preheat your oven to 425 F. Line a baking dish with waxed paper. Brush the butter over the fish. In a food processor, combine the rest of the ingredients. Coat the sea bass with the hazelnut mixture.

2. Place in the oven, and cook, for about 15 minutes.

Per Serving Calories 467, Net Carbs 2.8g, Fat 31g, Protein 40g

VEGAN AND VEGETARIAN

Cauliflower, Cheese and Collard Greens Waffles

SERVES: 4 | **PREPARATION TIME**: 45 MINUTES

Ingredients

2 green onions

1 tbsp olive oil

2 eggs

1/3 cup Parmesan cheese

1 cup collard greens

1 cup mozzarella cheese

½ cauliflower head

1 tsp garlic powder

1 tbsp sesame seeds

2 tsp thyme, chopped

Directions

1. Place the chopped cauliflower in the food processor and process until rice is formed.

2. Add collard greens, spring onions, and thyme to the food processor. Pulse until smooth. Transfer to a bowl.

3. Stir in the rest of the ingredients and mix to combine.

4. Heat your waffle iron and spread the mixture onto the iron, evenly.

5. Cook following the manufacturer's instructions.

Per Serving Calories 283, Net Carbs 3.5g, Fat 20.3g, Protein 16g

Strawberry & Spinach Salad with Goat Cheese

SERVES: 2 | **PREPARATION TIME**: 25 MINUTES

Ingredients

4 cups spinach

4 strawberries, sliced

½ cup almonds, flaked

1 ½ cups hard goat cheese, grated

4 tbsp raspberry vinaigrette

Salt and black pepper to taste

Directions

1. Preheat your oven to 400 F.
2. Arrange the grated goat cheese in two circles on two pieces of parchment paper. Place in the oven, and bake for 10 minutes.
3. Find two same bowls, place them upside down, and carefully put the parchment paper on top of them, to give the cheese a bowl-like shape.
4. Let cool that way for 15 minutes. Divide the spinach between the bowls.
5. Drizzle the vinaigrette over. Top with almonds and strawberries.

Per Serving Calories 645, Net Carbs 5.8g, Fat 54g, Protein 33g

Spinach & Feta Frittata

SERVES: 4 | **PREPARATION TIME**: 35 MINUTES

Ingredients

5 ounces spinach

8 ounces feta cheese, crumbled

1 pint cherry tomatoes, halved

10 eggs

3 tbsp olive oil

4 scallions, diced

Salt and black pepper to taste

Directions

1. Preheat your oven to 350 F.
2. Drizzle the oil in a 2-quart casserole and place in the oven until heated.
3. In a bowl, whisk the eggs along with the pepper and salt until thoroughly combined.
4. Stir in the spinach, feta cheese, and scallions.
5. Pour the mixture into the casserole, top with the cherry tomatoes, and place back in the oven. Bake for 25 minutes until your frittata is set in the middle.
6. When done, remove the casserole from the oven, and run a spatula around the edges of the frittata, slide it onto a warm platter.
7. Cut the frittata into wedges, and serve with salad.

Per Serving Calories 461, Net Carbs 6g, Fat 35g, Protein 26g

Spanish-Style Tomato Soup

SERVES: 6 | **PREPARATION TIME**: 15 MINUTES

Ingredients

2 small green peppers, roasted

2 large red peppers, roasted

2 medium avocados, flesh scoped out

2 garlic cloves

2 spring onions, chopped

1 cucumber, chopped

1 cup olive oil

2 tbsp lemon juice

4 tomatoes, chopped

7 ounces goat cheese

1 small red onion, coarsely chopped

2 tbsp apple cider vinegar

Salt to taste

Directions

1. Place the peppers, tomatoes, avocado, spring onions, garlic, lemon juice, olive oil, vinegar, and salt in a food processor or a blender.

2. Pulse until your desired consistency is reached. Taste, and adjust the seasoning.

3. Transfer the mixture to a pot. Stir in cucumbers and red onion. Cover and chill in the fridge at least 2 hours.

4. Divide the soup between 6 bowls. Serve very cold, generously topped with goat cheese and an extra drizzle of olive oil.

Per Serving Calories 528, Net Carbs 8.5g, Fat 45.8g, Protein 7.5g

Thyme Mushroom Soup

SERVES: 4 | **PREPARATION TIME**: 25 MINUTES

Ingredients

¼ cup butter

5 ounces crème fraiche

12 ounces wild mushrooms, chopped

2 tsp thyme leaves

2 garlic cloves, minced

4 cups vegetable broth

Salt and black pepper to taste

Directions

1. Melt the butter in a large pot over medium heat. Add garlic and cook for one minute until tender.
2. Add mushrooms, season with salt and pepper, and cook for 10 minutes.
3. Pour the broth over and bring to a boil. Reduce the heat and simmer for 10 minutes.
4. Blitz the soup with a hand blender until smooth. Stir in crème Fraiche.
5. Garnish with thyme leaves before serving.

Per Serving Calories 281, Net Carbs 5.8g, Fat 25g, Protein 6g

Mini Pepper Pizzas

SERVES: 2 | **PREPARATION TIME**: 40 MINUTES

Ingredients

6 ounces mozzarella

2 tbsp cream cheese

2 tbsp Parmesan cheese

1 tsp oregano

½ cup almond flour

2 tbsp psyllium husk

Toppings:

4 ounces cheddar cheese, grated

¼ cup marinara sauce

1 bell pepper, sliced

1 tomato, sliced

2 tbsp basil, chopped

Directions

1. Preheat the oven to 400 F.
2. Combine all of the crust ingredients in a large bowl, except the mozzarella.
3. Melt the mozzarella in a microwave. Stir it into the bowl.
4. Mix with your hands to combine. Divide the dough in two.
5. Roll out the two crusts in circles, and place on a lined baking sheet. Bake for about 10 minutes. Top with the toppings. Return to the oven, and bake for 10 minutes.

Per Serving Calories 510, Net Carbs 3.7g, Fat 39g, Protein 31g

Broccoli and Spinach Soup

SERVES: 6 | **PREPARATION TIME**: 30 MINUTES

s

1 broccoli head, chopped
7 ounces spinach
1 onion, chopped
2 garlic cloves, minced
5 ounces watercress
4 cups veggie stock

1 cup coconut milk
1 tsp salt
1 tbsp olive oil
1 bay leaf
Salt and black pepper to taste

Directions

1. Melt the olive oil in a large pot over medium heat. Add onion and cook for 3 minutes. Add garlic and cook for another minute. Add broccoli and cook for an additional 5 minutes.

2. Pour the stock over and add the bay leaf. Close the lid, bring to a boil, and reduce the heat. Simmer for about 3 minutes.

3. In the end, add spinach and watercress, and cook for 3 more minutes.

4. Stir in the coconut cream and salt and pepper. Discard the bay leaf, and blend the soup with a hand blender.

Per Serving Calories 392, Net Carbs 5.8g, Fat 37.6g, Protein 4.9g

Mac and Cheese Balls

SERVES: 7 | **PREPARATION TIME**: 45 MINUTES

Ingredients

1 cauliflower head, riced in a food processor
1 ½ cups cheese, shredded
2 tsp paprika

¾ tsp rosemary
2 tsp turmeric
3 eggs
Olive oil, for frying

Directions

1. Microwave the cauliflower for 5 minutes.
2. Place it in cheesecloth and squeeze the extra juices out.
3. Place the cauliflower in a bowl. Stir in the rest of the ingredients.
4. Heat the oil in a deep pan until it reaches 360 F.
5. Add the 'mac and cheese', and fry until golden and crispy. Drain on paper towels before serving.

Per Serving Calories 160, Net Carbs 2g, Fat 12g, Protein 8.6g

Broccoli Soup with Mint and Cheddar

SERVES: 4 | **PREPARATION TIME**: 20 MINUTES

Ingredients

¾ cup heavy cream

1 onion, diced

1 tsp garlic, minced

4 cups broccoli, chopped

4 cups veggie broth

2 tbsp butter

2 ¾ cups cheddar cheese + ¼ cup to garnish, grated

Salt and black pepper to taste

½ bunch fresh mint, chopped

Directions

1. Melt the butter in a large pot over medium heat.
2. Sauté onion and garlic for 3 minutes, or until nice, and tender stirring periodically. Season with salt and pepper. Add the broth, broccoli, and bring to a boil.
3. Reduce the heat and simmer for 10 minutes.
4. Blitz the soup with a hand blender until smooth.
5. Add in the cheese, and cook until creamy, about 1 minute.
6. Taste, season with salt and pepper. Stir in the heavy cream.
7. Serve in bowls with the reserved grated Cheddar cheese over, and sprinkled with the fresh mint. Yummy!

Per Serving Calories 561, Net Carbs 7g, Fat 52.3g, Protein 24g

Savory Vegetarian Burgers

SERVES: 2 | **PREPARATION TIME**: 20 MINUTES

Ingredients

1 garlic cloves, minced

2 portobello mushrooms, sliced

1 tbsp coconut oil, melted

1 tbsp basil, chopped

2 eggs, fried

4 low-carb bread slices

2 tbsp mayonnaise

2 lettuce leaves

Directions

1. Combine the melted coconut oil, garlic, basil, and salt in a bowl. Place in the mushrooms and coat well.

2. Preheat the grill to medium. Grill the mushrooms about 2 minutes per side.

3. To the two bread slices, add the lettuce leaves, then grilled mushrooms, then the eggs and finally the mayonnaise. Top with the other two slices.

Per Serving Calories 637, Net Carbs 8.5g, Fat 55g, Protein 23g

Baked Stuffed Portabello Mushrooms

SERVES: 2 | **PREPARATION TIME**: 30 MINUTES

Ingredients

4 portobello mushrooms

2 tbsp olive oil

2 cups lettuce

1 cup blue cheese, crumbled

Directions

1. Preheat your oven to 350 F. Remove the stems from the mushrooms.

2. Fill the mushrooms with blue cheese, and place on a lined baking sheet. Bake for about 20 minutes. Serve with lettuce drizzled with olive oil.

Per Serving Calories 334, Net Carbs 5.5g, Fat 29g, Protein 14g

Avocado & Pesto Zucchini Noodles

SERVES: 4 | **PREPARATION TIME**: 15 MINUTES

Ingredients

4 zucchini, julienne or spiralizer

½ cup pesto

2 avocados, sliced

1 cup Kalamata olives, chopped

¼ cup basil, chopped

2 tbsp olive oil

¼ cup sun-dried tomatoes, chopped

Directions

1. Heat half of the olive oil in a pan over medium heat. Add noodles, and cook for 4 minutes. Transfer to a plate.

2. Stir in olive oil, pesto, basil, salt, tomatoes and olives. Top with avocado slices.

Per Serving Calories 449, Net Carbs 8.4g, Fat 42g, Protein 6.3g

Speedy Grilled Cheese

SERVES: 1 | **PREPARATION TIME**: 15 MINUTES

Ingredients

2 eggs

½ tsp baking powder

2 tbsp butter

2 tbsp almond flour

1 ½ tbsp psyllium husk powder

2 ounces cheddar cheese

Directions

1. Whisk together all of the ingredients except 1 tbsp butter and cheddar.

2. Place in a square oven-proof bowl, and microwave for 90 seconds. Flip bun over and cut in half. Place the cheddar on one half of the bun and top with the other half.

3. Melt the remaining butter in a skillet. Add the sandwich, and grill until the cheese is melted and the bun is crispy.

Per Serving Calories 623, Net Carbs 6.4g, Fat 51g, Protein 25g

Three-Color Salad with Pesto Sauce

SERVES: 4 | **PREPARATION TIME**: 10 MINUTES

Ingredients

3 tomatoes, sliced

1 large avocado, sliced

8 kalamata olives

¼ pound buffalo mozzarella cheese, sliced

2 tbsp pesto sauce

2 tbsp olive oil

Directions

1. Arrange the tomato slices on a serving platter. Place the avocado slices in the middle. Arrange the olives around the avocado slices.

2. Drop pieces of mozzarella on the platter.

3. Drizzle the pesto sauce all over, and drizzle olive oil as well.

Per Serving Calories 290, Net Carbs 4.3g, Fat 25g, Protein 9g

Mushroom Risotto with Cheese

SERVES: 4 | **PREPARATION TIME**: 15 MINUTES

Ingredients

2 shallots, diced

3 tbsp olive oil

¼ cup veggie broth

1/3 cup Parmesan cheese

4 tbsp butter

3 tbsp chives, chopped

2 pounds mushrooms, sliced

4 ½ cups cauliflower, riced

Directions

1. Heat 2 tbsp. oil in a saucepan. Add the mushrooms, and cook over medium heat for about 3 minutes. Remove from the pan and set aside.

2. Heat the remaining oil, and cook the shallots for 2 minutes. Stir in the cauliflower and broth, and cook until the liquid is absorbed. Stir in the rest of the ingredients.

Per Serving Calories 264, Net Carbs 8.4g, Fat 18g, Protein 11g

SIDES AND SNACKS

Easy Bacon and Zucchini Hash

SERVES: 1 | **PREPARATION TIME**: 25 MINUTES

Ingredients

1 medium zucchini, diced
2 bacon slices
1 egg
1 tbsp coconut oil
½ small onion, chopped
1 tbsp parsley, chopped
¼ tsp salt

Directions

1. Place the bacon in a skillet and cook over medium heat for a few minutes, until the bacon is crispy. Remove from the skillet, and set aside.
2. Warm the coconut oil, and cook the onion until soft for about 3-4 minutes, stirring occasionally.
3. Add the zucchini, and cook for 10 more minutes until zucchini is brown, and tender, but not mushy. Transfer to a plate, and season with salt.
4. Crack the egg into the same skillet and fry it over medium heat.
5. Top the zucchini mixture with the bacon slices and a fried egg.
6. Serve hot, sprinkled with parsley.

Per Serving Calories 423, Net Carbs 6.6g, Fat 35.5g, Protein 17.4g

Stuffed Peppers with Goat Cheese & Garlic

SERVES: 8 | **PREPARATION TIME**: 15 MINUTES

Ingredients

8 canned piquillo peppers, roasted

1 tbsp olive oil

3 slices prosciutto, cut into thin slices

1 tbsp balsamic vinegar

Filling

8 ounces goat cheese

3 tbsp heavy cream

3 tbsp parsley, chopped

½ tsp garlic, minced

1 tbsp olive oil

1 tbsp mint, chopped

Directions

1. Combine all of the filling ingredients in a bowl.

2. Place the mixture in a freezer bag, press down and squeeze, and cut off the bottom.

3. Drain and deseed the peppers.

4. Squeeze about 2 tbsp. of the filling into each pepper.

5. Wrap a prosciutto slice onto each pepper. Secure with toothpicks.

6. Arrange them on a serving platter. Sprinkle the olive oil and vinegar over.

Per Serving Calories 110, Net Carbs 2.5g, Fat 9g, Protein 6g

Italian Sausage Pie with Eggplant & Tomatoes

SERVES: 6 | **PREPARATION TIME**: 55 MINUTES

Ingredients

6 eggs

12 oz raw sausage rolls

10 cherry tomatoes, halved

2 tbsp heavy cream

2 tbsp Parmesan cheese

¼ tsp salt

A pinch of black pepper

2 tbsp parsley, chopped

5 eggplant slices

Cooking spray

Directions

1. Preheat your oven to 375 F.
2. Grease a pie dish (preferably an 8-inch one) with cooking spray.
3. Press the sausage roll at the bottom of a pie dish.
4. Arrange the eggplant slices on top of the sausage. Top with cherry tomatoes.
5. Whisk together the eggs along with the heavy cream, salt, Parmesan cheese, and black pepper.
6. Spoon the egg mixture over the sausage.
7. Bake for about 40 minutes until it is browned around the edges.
8. Serve warm, and scatter with chopped parsley.

Per Serving Calories 340, Net Carbs 3g, Fat 28g, Protein 1.7g

Homemade Cheesy Spinach Balls

SERVES: 8 | **PREPARATION TIME**: 30 MINUTES

Ingredients

1/3 cup ricotta cheese, crumbled

¼ tsp nutmeg

¼ tsp pepper

3 tbsp heavy cream

1 tsp garlic powder

1 tbsp onion powder

2 tbsp butter, melted

1/3 cup Parmesan cheese

2 eggs

8 ounces spinach

1 cup almond flour

Directions

1. Place all of the ingredients in a food processor. Process until smooth.
2. Place in the freezer for about 10 minutes.
3. Make balls out of the mixture and arrange them on a lined baking sheet.
4. Bake at 350 F for about 10-12 minutes.

Per Serving Calories 60, Net Carbs 0.8g, Fat 5g, Protein 2g

Baked Ham & Cheese Egg Cakes

SERVES: 9 | **PREPARATION TIME**: 35 MINUTES

Ingredients

2 cups ham, chopped

1/3 cup Parmesan cheese, grated

1 tbsp parsley, chopped

¼ cup almond flour

9 eggs

1/3 cup mayonnaise, sugar-free

¼ tsp garlic powder

¼ cup onion, chopped

Sea salt to taste

Cooking spray

Directions

1. Preheat your oven to 375 F.
2. Lightly grease nine muffin pans with cooking spray, and set aside.
3. Place the onion, ham, garlic powder, and salt, in a food processor, and pulse until ground. Stir in the mayonnaise, almond flour, and Parmesan cheese.
4. Press this mixture into the muffin cups.
5. Make sure it goes all the way up the muffin sides so that there will be room for the egg. Bake for 5 minutes. Crack an egg into each muffin cup.
6. Return to the oven and bake for 20 more minutes or until the tops are firm to the touch and eggs are cooked.
7. Leave to cool slightly before serving, and serve right now. Enjoy!

Per Serving Calories 267, Net Carbs 1g, Fat 18g, Protein 13.5g

Easy Salad with Bacon and Avocado

SERVES: 4 | **PREPARATION TIME**: 20 MINUTES

Ingredients

2 large avocados, 1 chopped and 1 sliced

1 spring onion, sliced

4 cooked bacon slices, crumbled

2 cups spinach

2 small lettuce heads, chopped

2 hardboiled eggs, chopped

<u>**Vinaigrette**</u>

3 tbsp olive oil   1 tbsp apple cider vinegar

1 tsp Dijon mustard

Directions

1. Combine the spinach, lettuce, eggs, chopped avocados, and spring onion in a bowl.
2. Whisk together the vinaigrette ingredients in another bowl.
3. Pour the dressing over. Toss to combine. Top with the sliced avocado and bacon.
4. Serve and enjoy!

Tip: Top with blue cheese, for a touch more extra flavor and calories.

Per Serving Calories 350, Net Carbs 3.4g, Fat 33g, Protein 7g

Greek Salad with Capers

SERVES: 4 | **PREPARATION TIME**: 10 MINUTES

Ingredients

5 tomatoes, chopped   4 tbsp capers

1 large cucumber, chopped   7 ounces feta cheese, chopped

1 green bell pepper, chopped   1 tsp oregano, dried

1 small red onion, chopped   4 tbsp olive oil

16 Kalamata olives, chopped   Salt to taste

Directions

1. Place tomatoes, pepper, cucumber, onion, feta and olives in a bowl.
2. Mix to combine well. Season with salt.
3. Combine the capers, olive oil and oregano in a small bowl.
4. Drizzle the dressing over the salad.

Per Serving Calories 323, Net Carbs 8g, Fat 28g, Protein 9.3g

Garlic & Herbed Buttered Eggs

Ingredients

1 tbsp coconut oil

2 tbsp butter

1 tsp fresh thyme

4 eggs

2 garlic cloves, minced

½ cup parsley, chopped

½ cup cilantro, chopped

¼ tsp cumin

¼ tsp cayenne pepper

Salt and black pepper to taste

Directions

1. Drizzle the coconut oil into a non-stick skillet over medium heat.

2. Once the oil is warm, add the butter, leave to melt.

3. Add garlic and thyme and cook for 30 seconds.

4. Sprinkle with parsley and cilantro, and cook for another 2-3 minutes, until crisp.

5. Carefully crack the eggs into the skillet.

6. Lower the heat and cook for 4-6 minutes. Adjust the seasoning.

7. When the eggs are just set, turn the heat off and transfer to a serving plate.

8. Serve warm.

Per Serving Calories 321, Net Carbs 2.5g, Fat 21.5g, Protein 12.8g

Cauliflower Salad with Shrimp and Cucumber

SERVES: 6 | **PREPARATION TIME**: 30 MINUTES

Ingredients

1 cauliflower head, florets only

1 pound medium shrimp

¼ cup + 1 tbsp olive oil

2 cucumber, peeled and chopped

3 tbsp dill, chopped

¼ cup lemon juice

2 tbsp lemon zest

Directions

1. Heat 1 tbsp. olive oil in a skillet, and cook the shrimp until opaque, about 8-10 minutes.
2. Place the cauliflower florets in a microwave-safe bowl, and microwave for 5 minutes.
3. Place the shrimp, cauliflower, and cucumber in a large bowl.
4. Whisk together the remaining olive oil, lemon zest, lemon juice, dill, and some salt and pepper in another bowl.
5. Pour the dressing over. Toss to combine.
6. Serve immediately.

Per Serving Calories 214, Net Carbs 5g, Fat 17g, Protein 15g

Bacon with Mozzarella and Tomato Salad

SERVES: 2 | **PREPARATION TIME**: 10 MINUTES

Ingredients

1 large tomato, sliced

4 basil leaves

8 mozzarella cheese slices

2 tsp olive oil

3 ounces bacon, chopped

1 tsp balsamic vinegar

Sea salt to taste

Directions

1. Place the bacon in a skillet over medium heat and cook until crispy.
2. Divide the tomato slices between two serving plates.
3. Arrange the mozzarella slices over. Top with the basil leaves.
4. Add the crispy bacon on top.
5. Drizzle with olive oil and vinegar.
6. Sprinkle with sea salt and serve.

Per Serving Calories 279, Net Carbs 1.5g, Fat 26g, Protein 21g

Muffin Breakfast Sandwiches

SERVES: 2 | **PREPARATION TIME**: 5 MINUTES

Ingredients

¼ cup flax meal

1 egg

2 tbsp heavy cream

2 tbsp pesto

¼ cup almond flour

¼ tsp baking soda

Salt and black pepper to taste

Filling

2 tbsp cream cheese

4 slices of bacon

½ medium avocado, sliced

Directions

1. Mix together the dry muffin ingredients in a bowl. Add egg, heavy cream, and pesto, and whisk well with a fork. Season with salt and pepper. Divide the mixture between two ramekins. Place in the microwave and cook for 60-90 seconds. Leave to cool before filling.

2. Meanwhile, in a nonstick skillet, over medium heat, cook the bacon slices until crispy. Transfer to paper towels to soak up excess fat. Set aside.

3. Invert the muffins onto a plate and cut in half, crosswise.

4. Make sandwiches by spreading cream cheese and topping with bacon and avocado.

Per Serving Calories 511, Net Carbs 4.5g, Fat 38.2g, Protein 16.4g

Quick Browned Butter Broccoli

SERVES: 6 | **PREPARATION TIME**: 10 MINUTES

Ingredients

1 broccoli head, florets only

¼ cup butter

Salt to taste

Directions

1. Place the broccoli in a pot filled with salted water, and bring to a boil. Cook for about 3 minutes, or until tender. Melt the butter in a microwave.

2. Drain the broccoli and transfer to a plate. Drizzle the butter over and season with some salt and pepper.

Per Serving Calories 114, Net Carbs 5.5g, Fat 7.8g, Protein 3.9g

Chicken Prosciutto & Provolone Wraps

SERVES: 8 | **PREPARATION TIME**: 20 MINUTES

Ingredients

¼ tsp garlic powder

8 ounces provolone cheese

8 raw chicken tenders

⅛ tsp black pepper

8 prosciutto slices

Directions

1. Pound the chicken until half an inch thick. Season with salt, pepper, and garlic powder.

2. Cut the provolone cheese into 8 strips.

3. Place a slice of prosciutto on a flat surface.

4. Place one chicken tender on top. Top with a provolone strip.

5. Roll the chicken, and secure with previously soaked skewers.

6. Preheat the grill.

7. Grill the wraps for about 3 minutes per side.

Per Serving Calories 174, Net Carbs 0.8g, Fat 10g, Protein 17g

Savory Fried Artichoke Hearts

Ingredients

12 fresh baby artichokes

2 tbsp lemon juice

2 tbsp olive oil

Salt to taste

Directions

1. Slice the artichokes vertically into narrow wedges.
2. Drain them on paper towels before frying.
3. Heat the olive oil in a cast-iron skillet over high heat.
4. Fry the artichokes until browned and crispy.
5. Drain excess oil on paper towels. Sprinkle with salt and lemon juice.

Per Serving Calories 35, Net Carbs 2.9g, Fat 2.4g, Protein 2g

Tabasco & Mayonnaise Deviled Eggs

Ingredients

6 eggs

1 tbsp green tabasco

1/3 cup sugar-free mayonnaise

Directions

1. Place the eggs in a saucepan, and cover with salted water. Bring to a boil over medium heat. Boil for 8 minutes.
2. Place the eggs in an ice bath and let cool for 10 minutes. Peel and slice them in.
3. Whisk together the tabasco, mayonnaise, and salt in a small bowl. Spoon this mixture on top of every egg.

Per Serving Calories 178, Net Carbs 5g, Fat 17g, Protein 6g

Friday Night Cauliflower Fritters

SERVES: 4 | **PREPARATION TIME**: 35 MINUTES

Ingredients

1 pound cauliflower, grated

½ cup Parmesan cheese

3 ounces onion, finely chopped

½ tsp baking powder

½ cup almond flour

3 eggs

½ tsp lemon juice

Olive oil, for frying

Directions

1. Sprinkle the salt over the cauliflower in a bowl, and let it stand for 10 minutes.
2. Place the other ingredients in the bowl. Mix with your hands to combine.
3. Put a skillet over medium heat, and heat some olive oil in it.
4. Meanwhile, shape fritters out of the cauliflower mixture.
5. Fry in batches for about 3 minutes per side.

Per Serving Calories 69, Net Carbs 3g, Fat 5.3g, Protein 4.5g

Prosciutto Wrapped Mozzarella Rolls

SERVES: 6 | **PREPARATION TIME**: 15 MINUTES

Ingredients

6 thin prosciutto slices

18 basil leaves

18 mozzarella ciliegine (about 8 ½ ounces in total)

Directions

1. Cut the prosciutto slices into three strips.
2. Place basil leaves at the end of each strip. Top with mozzarella.
3. Wrap the mozzarella in prosciutto. Secure with toothpicks.

Per Serving Calories 163, Net Carbs 0.5g, Fat 12g, Protein 13g

Party Bacon and Pistachio Liverwurst Truffles

SERVES: 8 | **PREPARATION TIME**: 45 MINUTES

Ingredients

8 bacon slices, cooked and chopped

8 ounces Liverwurst

¼ cup pistachios, chopped

1 tsp Dijon mustard

6 ounces cream cheese

Directions

1. Combine the liverwurst and pistachios in the bowl of your food processor.
2. Pulse until smooth. Whisk the cream cheese and mustard in another bowl.
3. Make 12 balls out of the liverwurst mixture.
4. Make a thin cream cheese layer over. Coat with bacon pieces.
5. Arrange on a plate and refrigerate for 30 minutes.

Per Serving Calories 145, Net Carbs 1.5g, Fat 12g, Protein 7g

DESSERTS

Chocolate Peanut Butter Ice Cream Bars

SERVES: 15 | **PREPARATION TIME**: 4 HOURS AND 20 MINUTES

Ingredients

1 cup heavy whipping cream

1 tsp vanilla extract

¾ tsp xanthan gum

1/3 cup peanut butter

1 cup half and half

1 ½ cups almond milk

1/3 tsp stevia powder

1 tbsp vegetable glycerin

3 tbsp xylitol

Chocolate:

¾ cup coconut oil

¼ cup cocoa butter pieces, chopped

2 ounces chocolate, unsweetened

3 ½ tsp super sweet blend

Directions

1. Blend all of the ice cream ingredients until smooth.
2. Place in an ice cream maker and follow the instructions.
3. Spread the ice cream into a lined pan, and freeze for about 4 hours.
4. Combine all of the chocolate ingredients in a microwave-safe bowl and microwave until melted. Slice the ice cream bars.
5. Dip them into the cooled chocolate mixture.

Per Serving Calories 345 Net Carbs 5g, Fat 32g, Protein 4g

Cinnamon Snickerdoodle Cookies

SERVES: 4 | **PREPARATION TIME**: 25 MINUTES

Ingredients

2 cups almond flour

½ tsp baking soda

¾ cup sweetener

½ cup butter softened

A pinch of salt

Coating:

2 tbsp erythritol sweetener

1 tsp cinnamon

Directions

1. Preheat your oven to 350 F.
2. Combine all of the cookie ingredients in a bowl. Make 16 balls out of the mixture.
3. Flatten them with your hands. Combine the cinnamon and erythritol.
4. Dip the cookies in the cinnamon mixture and arrange them on a lined cookie sheet.
5. Bake for 15 minutes.

Per Serving Calories 131, Net Carbs 1.5g, Fat 13g, Protein 3g

Lemon Cheesecake with Raspberry

SERVES: 12 | **PREPARATION TIME**: 4 HOURS AND 50 MINUTES

Ingredients

2 egg whites

¼ cup erythritol

3 cups coconut, desiccated

1 tsp coconut oil

¼ cup butter, melted

Filling:

3 tbsp lemon juice

6 ounces raspberries

2 cups erythritol

1 cup whipped cream

Zest of 1 lemon

3 tbsp lemon juice

24 ounces cream cheese

Directions

1. Apply the coconut oil to the bottom and sides of a springform pan.
2. Line with parchment paper. Preheat your oven to 350 F.
3. Mix all of the crust ingredients, and pour the crust into the pan. Bake for about 25 minutes. Let cool.
4. Meanwhile, beat the cream cheese until soft. Add the lemon juice, zest, and sweetener. In a mixing bowl, beat the heavy cream with an electric mixer.
5. Fold the whipped cream into the cheese cream mixture. Fold in the raspberries gently. Spoon the filling into the baked and cooled crust.
6. Refrigerate for 4 hours before serving.

Per Serving Calories 215, Net Carbs 3 g, Fat 25 g, Protein 5 g

Chocolate Delight of Cream & Strawberries

SERVES: 4 | **PREPARATION TIME**: 30 MINUTES

Ingredients

3 eggs
1 cup dark chocolate chips
1 cup heavy cream

1 cup fresh strawberries, sliced
1 vanilla extract
1 tbsp swerve

Directions

1. Melt the chocolate in a microwave-safe bowl in your microwave for a minute on high, and let it cool for 10 minutes.
2. Meanwhile, in a medium-sized mixing bowl whip the cream until very soft.
3. Add the eggs, vanilla extract, and swerve and whisk to combine. Fold int the cooled chocolate.
4. Divide the mousse between six glasses, top with the strawberry slices and chill in the fridge for at least 30 minutes before serving.

Per Serving Calories 410, Net Carbs 1.7g, Fat 25g, Protein 7.6g

Awesome Berry Tart

SERVES: 4 | **PREPARATION TIME**: 45 MINUTES

Ingredients

4 eggs

2 tsp coconut oil

2 cups berries

1 cup coconut milk

1 cup almond flour

¼ cup sweetener

½ tsp vanilla powder

1 tbsp sweetener, powdered

A pinch of salt

Directions

1. Preheat the oven to 350 F.
2. Lace all of the ingredients except the coconut oil, berries, and powdered sweetener in a blender. Blend until smooth. Gently fold in the berries.
3. Grease a flan dish with the coconut oil. Pour the mixture into the prepared pan.
4. Bake for 35 minutes. Sprinkle with powdered sugar and serve.

Per Serving Calories 198, Net Carbs 4.9g, Fat 16.5g, Protein 15g

Lemon Apple Pie

SERVES: 8 | **PREPARATION TIME**: 65 MINUTES

Ingredients

Crust:

6 tbsp butter

2 cups almond flour

1 tsp cinnamon

1/3 cup sweetener

Filling:

2 cups sliced granny smith

¼ cup butter

¼ cup sweetener

½ tsp cinnamon

½ tsp lemon juice

Topping:

¼ tsp cinnamon   2 tbsp sweetener

Directions

1. Preheat your oven to 375 F. Combine all of the crust ingredients in a bowl.
2. Press the mixture into the bottom of a greased pan. Bake for 5 minutes.
3. Meanwhile, combine the apples and lemon juice in a bowl, and let them sit until the crust is ready. Arrange them on top of the crust.
4. Combine the rest of the filling ingredients, and brush this mixture over the apples. Bake for about 30 minutes.
5. Press the apples down with a spatula, return to oven, and bake for 20 more minutes.
6. Combine the cinnamon and sweetener and sprinkle over the tart.

Per Serving Calories 302, Net Carbs 6.7g, Fat 26g, Protein 7g

Blackberries Chia Seed Pudding

SERVES: 2 | **PREPARATION TIME**: 35 MINUTES

Ingredients

1 cup full-fat natural yogurt   1 cup fresh blackberries

2 tsp swerve   1 tbsp lemon zest

2 tbsp chia seeds   Mint leaves, to serve

Directions

1. Mix together the yogurt and the swerve. Stir in the chia seeds.
2. Reserve 4 blackberries for garnish and mash the remaining blackberries with a fork until pureed. Stir in the yogurt mixture
3. Chill in the fridge for 30 minutes.
4. When cooled, divide the mixture into 2 glasses.
5. Top each with a couple of raspberries and mint leaves and serve.

Per Serving Calories 169, Net Carbs 1.7g, Fat 10g, Protein 7.6g

Creamy Almond Butter Smoothie

Ingredients

1 ½ cups almond milk

2 tbsp almond butter

⅛ tsp almond extract

½ tsp cinnamon

2 tbsp flax meal

1 scoop collagen peptides

A pinch of salt

15 drops of stevia

A handful of ice cubes

Directions

1. Add almond milk, almond butter, flax meal, almond extract, collagen peptides, a pinch of salt, and stevia to the bowl of your blender.
2. Blitz until uniform and smooth for about 30 seconds.
3. Add a bit more almond milk if it's very thick.
4. Then taste, and adjust flavor as needed, adding more stevia for sweetness or almond butter to the creaminess.
5. Pour into your smoothie glass, add the ice cubes and sprinkle with cinnamon.
6. Enjoy!

Per Serving Calories 326, Net Carbs 6g, Fat 27g, Protein 19g

Porridge with Chia & Walnuts

Ingredients

½ tsp vanilla extract

½ cup water

1 tbsp chia seeds

2 tbsp hemp seeds

1 tbsp flaxseed meal

2 tbsp almond meal

2 tbsp coconut, shredded

¼ tsp stevia, granulated

1 tbsp walnuts, chopped

Directions

1. Put the chia seeds, hemp seeds, flaxseed meal, almond meal, granulated stevia, and shredded coconut in a nonstick saucepan, and pour over the water.
2. Simmer over medium heat, stirring occasionally, until creamed and thickened for about 3-4 minutes. Stir in vanilla.
3. When the porridge is ready, spoon into a serving bowl, sprinkle with chopped walnuts, and serve warm.

Per Serving Calories 334, Net Carbs 1.5g, Fat 29g, Protein 15g

Savory Cardamom Saffron Bars

SERVES: 4 | **PREPARATION TIME**: 3 HOURS

Ingredients

3 ½ ounces ghee

10 saffron threads

1 1/3 cups coconut milk

1 ¾ cups coconut, shredded

4 tbsp sweetener

1 tsp cardamom powder

Directions

1. Combine the coconut with 1 cup of the coconut milk.
2. In another bowl, mix together the remaining coconut milk with the sweetener and saffron.
3. Let sit for 30 minutes. Heat the ghee in a wok.
4. Add the coconut mixture as well as the saffron mixture, and cook for 5 minutes on low heat, while mixing continuously.
5. Stir in the cardamom, and cook for another 5 minutes.
6. Spread the mixture onto a greased baking pan.
7. Freeze for 2 hours. Cut into bars and enjoy!

Per Serving Calories 130, Net Carbs 1.4g, Fat 12g, Protein 2g

Mom's Pecan Cookies

SERVES: 12 | **PREPARATION TIME**: 25 MINUTES

Ingredients

1 egg

2 cups pecans, ground

¼ cup sweetener

½ tsp baking soda

1 tbsp butter

20 pecan halves

Directions

1. Preheat the oven to 350 F. Mix the ingredients, except the pecan halves, until combined.

2. Make 20 balls out of the mixture and press them with your thumb onto a lined cookie sheet.

3. Top each cookie with a pecan half. Bake for about 12 minutes.

Per Serving Calories 101, Net Carbs 0.6g, Fat 11g, Protein 1.6g

Mocha Ice Bombs

SERVES: 4 | **PREPARATION TIME**: 2 HOURS AND 10 MINUTES

Ingredients

½ pound cream cheese

4 tbsp d sweetener, powdered

2 ounces strong coffee

2 tbsp cocoa powder, unsweetened

1 ounce cocoa butter, melted

2 ½ ounces dark chocolate, melted

Directions

1. Combine cream cheese, sweetener, coffee, and cocoa powder in a food processor.

2. Roll 2 tbsp of the mixture and place on a lined tray.

3. Mix the cocoa butter and chocolate, and coat the bombs with it. Freeze for 2 hours.

Per Serving Calories 127, Net Carbs 1.4g, Fat 13g, Protein 1.9g

Dark Chocolate Almond Bark

Ingredients

½ cup almonds

½ cup coconut butter

10 drops stevia

¼ tsp salt

½ cup coconut flakes, unsweetened

4 ounces dark chocolate

Directions

1. Preheat the oven to 350 F.
2. Place the almonds in a baking sheet, and toast for 5 minutes.
3. Melt together the butter and chocolate. Stir in stevia.
4. Line a cookie sheet with waxed paper and spread the chocolate evenly.
5. Scatter the almonds on top and sprinkle with salt.
6. Refrigerated for one hour.

Per Serving Calories 161, Net Carbs 2g, Fat 15.3g, Protein 2g

3-WEEK MEAL PLAN + SHOPPING LIST

MENU FOR WEEK ONE

MONDAY

Breakfast: Muffin Breakfast Sandwiches

Lunch: Spinach Hasselback Chicken

Snack: Friday Night Cauliflower Fritters (x4)

Dinner: Cotija Beef Burgers p.39

Per Day Calories: 1511; Net Carbs: 21g; Fat: 119.4g; Protein: 92.4g

TUESDAY

Breakfast: Garlic & Herbed Buttered Eggs

Lunch: Turkey Soup with Buffalo Sauce

Snack: Homemade Cheesy Spinach Balls

Dinner: Zucchini Stuffed with Beef, Onion & Cheese

Per Day Calories: 1542; Net Carbs: 20.9g; Fat: 115g; Protein: 73.3g

WEDNESDAY

Breakfast: Creamy Almond Butter Smoothie

Lunch: Thyme Mushroom Soup

Snack: Mocha Ice Bombs (x4)

Dinner: Cheese Beef Burgers with Cauli Rice Casserole

Per Day Calories: 1450; Net Carbs: 22.4g; Fat: 129g; Protein: 52.6g

THURSDAY

Breakfast: Blackberries Chia Seed Pudding

Lunch: Easy Salad with Bacon and Avocado

Snack: Homemade Cheesy Spinach Balls (x8)

Dinner: Garlic Lemon Pork Chops with Brussel Sprouts

Per Day Calories: 1548; Net Carbs: 13.5g; Fat: 131g; Protein: 56.6g

FRIDAY

Breakfast: Salmon Omelet with Avocado

Lunch: Greek Salad with Capers

Snack: Dark Chocolate Almond Bark

Dinner: Salmon Crusted with Pistachio Nuts and Sauce

Per Day Calories: 1561; Net Carbs: 21.8g; Fat: 138.3g; Protein: 82.3g

SATURDAY

Breakfast: Cauliflower, Cheese and Collard Greens Waffles

Lunch: Strawberry & Spinach Salad with Goat Cheese

Snack: Chocolate Peanut Butter Ice Cream Bars

Dinner: Zucchini Stuffed with Beef, Onion & Cheese

Per Day Calories: 1608; Net Carbs: 21.3g; Fat: 130.3g; Protein: 71g

SUNDAY

Breakfast: Baked Ham & Cheese Egg Cakes

Lunch: Easy Salad with Bacon and Avocado

Snack: Chocolate Peanut Butter Ice Cream Bars (x2)

Dinner: Chicken Prosciutto & Provolone Wraps

Per Day Calories: 1481; Net Carbs: 15.2g; Fat: 125g; Protein: 45.5g

SHOPPING LIST FOR WEEK ONE

MEAT AND SEAFOOD

Pork loin chops (6)

Bacon (8 slices)

Ham (2 cups)

Prosciutto (8 slices)

Beef ground (4½ pounds)

Turkey (1½ pounds)

Chicken breast (3)

Chicken, tenders (8)

Salmon fillets (4)

Salmon, smoked (2 ounces)

DAIRY AND EGGS

Butter (3 cups)

Cream cheese (3 cups)

Half-and-half (1 cup)

Heavy cream (4 cups)

Creme Fraiche (5 ounces)

Ricotta cheese (1/3 cup)

Provolone cheese (8 oz)

Cotija cheese (1 cup)

Parmesan cheese (1½ cups)

Feta cheese (7 ounces)

Colby Jack, grated (1 cup)

Yellow cheddar (1 cup)

Mozzarella (2 1/3 cups)

Goat cheese (1½ cups)

Yogurt natural (1 cup)

Eggs (30)

Mayonnaise (½ cup)

VEGETABLES AND FRUITS

Cauli rice (3 cups)

Cabbage (½ head)

Spinach (10 cups)

Shallot (1)

Thyme, fresh (1 bunch)

Tomato (5)

Zucchini (8)

Brussel sprouts (1 Ib)

Wild mushrooms (12 oz)

Lettuce heads (4 heads)

Chives

Cauliflower (1 Ib)

Cucumber (1)

Collard greens (1 cup)

Garlic cloves (5)

Green bell pepper (1)

Lemons (3)

Onion (5)

Green onion (2)

Red onion (2)

Pimiento rojo (2)

Avocados (3)

Strawberries (4)

Blackberries fresh (1 cup)

Mint leaves

Parsley, fresh (1 bunch)

NUTS

Nutmeg (1/3 cup)

Almonds (½ cup)

Pistachios, chopped (½ cup)

Coconut flakes (½ cup)

OILS, FATS, NUTS, SPICES AND PANTRY ITEMS

Olive oil

Coconut oil

Cooking spray

Cocoa butter

Coconut butter (½ cup)

Peanut butter (1 cup)

Parsley, dried

Cilantro

Chia seeds (4tbsp)

Cumin

Cayenne pepper

Sesame seeds

Oregano

Black Pepper

Salt and Kosher Salt

Flax meal

Vinaigrette

Apple cider vinegar

Raspberry vinaigrette

Almond flour (1½ cups)

Baking soda

Baking powder

Sweetener powder

Stevia, powder

Cocoa powder

Liquid stevia extract

Vanilla extract

Vegetable glycerin

Thm super sweet blend

Swerve sugar

Xylitol

Dark chocolate (4 oz)

Chocolate (4 oz)

White wine (2 cups)

Tomatoes (1 can 14-oz)

Xanthan gum

Strong coffee

Almond flakes

OTHER

Almond flour buns (4)

Almond milk (2 cups)

Chicken broth (2 cups)

Vegetable broth (6 cups)

Tomato basil sauce (½ cup)

Pesto (5 tbsp)

Buffalo Sauce (1/3 cup)

Capers (5 tbsp)

Worchestershire sauce

Dijon mustard

Kalamata olives (16)

MENU FOR WEEK TWO

MONDAY

Breakfast: Muffin Breakfast Sandwiches

Lunch: Spicy Pork Lettuce Wraps

Snack: Chocolate Delight of Cream & Strawberries

Dinner: Spicy Pork with Peanut Butter & Veggies

Per Day Calories: 1603; Net Carbs: 8.2g; Fat: 116.5g; Protein: 65.5g

TUESDAY

Breakfast: Creamy Almond Butter Smoothie

Lunch: Cauliflower Salad with Shrimp and Cucumber

Snack: Mocha Ice Bombs (x4)

Dinner: Zucchini and Turkey Bolognese Pasta

Per Day Calories: 1321; Net Carbs: 20.4g; Fat: 112g; Protein: 60.6g

WEDNESDAY

Breakfast: Baked Ham & Cheese Egg Cakes (x2)

Lunch: Slow Cooked Sausage and Cheddar Beer Soup

Snack: Tabasco & Mayonnaise Deviled Eggs

Dinner: Skillet Browned Chicken with Creamy Greens

Per Day Calories: 1682; Net Carbs: 10,1g; Fat: 131g; Protein: 66g

THURSDAY

Breakfast: Ricotta with Squash and Sausage Omelet

Lunch: Greek Salad with Capers

Snack: Party Bacon and Pistachio Liverwurst Truffles (x3)

Dinner: Garlic Lemon Pork Chops with Brussel Sprouts

Per Day Calories: 1565; Net Carbs: 18g; Fat: 133.7g; Protein: 68.6g

FRIDAY

Breakfast: Porridge with Chia & Walnuts

Lunch: Bacon with Mozzarella and Tomato Salad

Snack: Chocolate Peanut Butter Ice Cream Bars

Dinner: Garlic Lemon Pork Chops with Brussel Sprouts

Per Day Calories: 1507; Net Carbs: 10g; Fat: 135g; Protein: 66g

SATURDAY

Breakfast: Garlic & Herbed Buttered Eggs

Lunch: Easy Bacon and Zucchini Hash

Snack: Cinnamon Snickerdoodle Cookies (x2)

Dinner: Tart with Meat and Mashed Cauliflower

Per Day Calories: 1491; Net Carbs: 16.1g; Fat: 124g; Protein: 65.2g

SUNDAY

Breakfast: Cauliflower, Cheese and Collard Greens Waffles

Lunch: Creamy Reuben Soup

Snack: Chocolate Peanut Butter Ice Cream Bars

Dinner: Flank Steak Pinwheels

Per Day Calories: 1568; Net Carbs: 18.5g; Fat: 110g; Protein: 71g

SHOPPING LIST FOR WEEK TWO

MEAT AND SEAFOOD

Pork ground (4 pounds)

Sausages (4 oz)

Corned beef (1 pound)

Bacon (20 slices)

Liverwurst (8 oz)

Turkey, ground (1½ pounds)

Pork loin (12 Ib)

Beef flank steak (1½ lb)

Chicken thighs (1 pound)

Ham (2 cups)

Beef sausages (10 ounces)

Shrimp, medium (1 pound)

DAIRY AND EGGS

Almond butter (½ cup)

Heavy cream (6 1/3 cups)

Ricotta cheese (¼ cup)

Butter (2 cups)

Cheddar cheese (1 cup)

Swiss cheese (1¼ cups)

Cocoa butter (2 oz)

Swiss cheese (½ cup)

Eggs (30)

Cream (1 cup)

Mozzarella cheese (8 slices)

Mayonnaise (1 cup)

Cream cheese (16 oz)

Mozzarella (1¼ cups)

Half-and-half (1 cup)

Parmesan cheese (1 cup)

VEGETABLES AND FRUITS

Cucumber (4)

Brussels sprouts (2 Ib)

Dark leafy greens (2 carp)

Cauliflower (2)

Lemons (1)

Celery

Kale(1 cup)

Onion green (4)

Cilantro (1 cup)

Collard greens (1 cup)

Onion (6)

Carrots (1 cup)

Tomatoes (6)

Onion red (1)

Garlic (12 cloves)

Vegetables stir-fry (2 cups)

Red bell pepper (1)

Thyme, fresh (1 bunch)

Mushrooms (2 cups)

Sauerkraut

Avocados (1)

Zucchini (2 cups)

Green bell pepper (1)

Strawberries (1 cup)

Basil, fresh (1 bunch)

Jalapeño pepper (1)

Squash (4 oz)

Lettuce iceberg (1 head)

Baby spinach (½ cup)

NUTS

Pistachios, chopped (¼ cup) Walnuts, chopped (1 tbsp)

OILS, SPICES AND PANTRY ITEMS

Olive oil

Coconut oil

Peanut butter

Ghee

Cumin

Thm super sweet blend

Cayenne pepper

Cinnamon

Sage

Allspice

Pepper

Salt

Pink salt

Chili pepper

Parsley

Garlic powder

Dill

Oregano

Red pepper flakes

Kosher salt

Cinnamon

Flax meal

Balsamic vinegar

Caraway seeds

Sesame seeds

Chia seeds

Hemp seeds

Almond extract

Vanilla extract

Baking soda

Cocoa powder

Coconut flour (½ cup)

Almond flour (2 cups)

Almond meal

Erythritol sweetener

Xanthan gum

Xylitol

Coconut, shredded

Liquid stevia extract

Swerve

Stevia granulated

Vegetable glycerin

Stevia powder

Sweetener, powder

Dark chocolate chips

Dark chocolate

Chocolate (2 oz)

Strong coffee

White wine

Beer (16 ounces)

Veggie pasta (6 cups)

OTHER

Collagen peptides

Kalamata olives (16)

Chicken broth (1 cup)

Almond milk (3 cups)

Green tabasco

Dijon mustard

Pesto (3 tbsp)

Ginger garlic paste

Capers (½ cup)

Beef stock (18 ounces)

Chicken broth (2 cups)

MENU FOR WEEK THREE

MONDAY

Breakfast: Garlic & Herbed Buttered Eggs

Lunch: Avocado & Pesto Zucchini Noodles

Snack: Mocha Ice Bombs (x3)

Dinner: Lamb Chops with Sage & White Wine

Per Day Calories: 1548; Net Carbs: 19.4g; Fat: 151.9g; Protein: 40.8g

TUESDAY

Breakfast: Salmon Omelet with Avocado
Lunch: Pork Chops with Raspberry Sauce

Snack: Dark Chocolate Almond Bark (x2)

Dinner: Zucchini Stuffed with Beef, Onion & Cheese

Per Day Calories: 1584; Net Carbs: 17.9g; Fat: 135.1g; Protein: 85.3g

WEDNESDAY

Breakfast: Muffin Breakfast Sandwiches

Lunch: Broccoli and Spinach Soup

Snack: Mom's Pecan Cookies (x4)

Dinner: Cauli Rice with Vegetables and Beef Steak

Per Day Calories: 1627; Net Carbs: 16.7g; Fat: 145.8g; Protein: 42.7g

THURSDAY

Breakfast: Blackberries Chia Seed Pudding (x2)

Lunch: Strawberry & Spinach Salad with Goat Cheese

Snack: Savory Cardamom Saffron Bars (x2)

Dinner: Cheese Beef Burgers with Cauli Rice Casserole

Per Day Calories: 1578; Net Carbs: 17g; Fat: 123g; Protein: 72.2g

FRIDAY

Breakfast: Baked Ham & Cheese Egg Cakes

Lunch: Creole Beef Tripe Stew

Snack: Cinnamon Snickerdoodle Cookies (x2)

Dinner: Bunless Beef Burgers with Sriracha

Per Day Calories: 1535; Net Carbs: 12.9g; Fat: 126g; Protein: 80.5g

SATURDAY

Breakfast: Creamy Almond Butter Smoothie

Lunch: Grandma's Meatloaf with Balsamic Glaze

Snack: Chocolate Peanut Butter Ice Cream Bars

Dinner: Garlic Lemon Pork Chops with Brussel Sprouts

Per Day Calories: 1484; Net Carbs: 19g; Fat: 126g; Protein: 72g

SUNDAY

Breakfast: Porridge with Chia & Walnuts (x2)

Lunch:Three-Color Salad with Pesto Sauce

Snack: Chocolate Delight of Cream & Strawberries

Dinner: Cauli Rice with Vegetables and Beef Steak

Per Day Calories: 1688; Net Carbs: 13g; Fat: 134g; Protein: 61.6g

SHOPPING LIST FOR WEEK THREE

MEAT AND SEAFOOD

Pork chops (3 lb)

Ground beef (8 pounds)

Lamb chops (6)

Bacon (4 slices)

Beef tripe (1 ½ lb)

Salmon smoked (2 oz)

Ham (2 cups)

Beef skirt steak (2 lb)

DAIRY AND EGGS

Butter (2 cups)

Heavy cream (4 cups)

Parmesan cheese (2 cups)

Buttermilk (4 cups)

Half-and-half (1 cup)

Colby Jack cheese (1 cup)

Cocoa butter (1½ ounces)

Yellow cheddar (1 cup)

Yogurt natural (1 cup)

Almond butter (2 tbsp)

Goat cheese hard (1½ cups)

Eggs (25)

Ghee (4 oz)

Buffalo mozzarella cheese, sliced (¼ pound)

Mayonnaise (2 cups)

Cream cheese (1 pound)

VEGETABLES AND FRUITS

Red onion (1)

Parsley, fresh (1 bunch)

Tomato (3)

Pimiento rojo (2 tbsp)

Basil

Zucchini (8)

Bell pepper (2)

Broccoli (1 head)

Cauli rice (2 cups)

Brussels sprouts (1 lb)

Slaw (6 tbsp)

Avocados (4)

Garlic cloves (17)

Spinach (8 ounces)

Raspberries (2 cups)

Lemon (1)

Wetercress (5 ounces)

Blackberries (1 cup)

Cabbage (2 cups)

Thyme, fresh (1 bunch)

Strawberries (2 cups)

Onion (7)

Cilantro

Mint leaves, fresh (1 bunch)

Spring onion (1)

Garlic powder

NUTS

Almonds

Pecans

Walnuts

OILS, SPICES AND PANTRY ITEMS

Olive oil

Coconut oil

Peanut butter

Cocoa butter pieces

Cocoa powder

Coconut, shredded

Almond flour (1 ½ cups)

Almond extract

Almond meal

Balsamic vinegar

Raspberry vinaigrette

Cinnamon

Tomato, diced (16 oz)

Saffron threads

Pink salt

Italian herb mix

Kosher salt

Cayenne pepper

Pepper

Salt

Onion powder

Garlic powder

Cardamom powder

Sage

Thyme

Sun-dried tomatoes (¼ cup)

Creole seasoning

Cumin

Vegetable glycerin

Erythritol sweetener

Sweetener, powder

Xylitol

Xantham gum

Liquid stevia extract

Thm super sweet blend

Swerve

Chia seeds

Hemp seeds

Flax meal

Coconut flakes

Vanilla extract

Chocolate, unsweetened

Dark chocolate

Dark chocolate chips

White wine

Strong coffee

Baking soda

OTHER

Sriracha

Almond milk (2 cups)

Worcestershire sauce

Pesto (3 tbsp)

Mixed vegetables

Veggie stock (5 cups)

Hot sauce (sugar-free)

Keto buns (4)

Dijon mustard

Chives (3 tbsp)

Kalamata olives (2 cups)

Collagen peptides

Coconut milk (3 cups)

Made in the USA
Columbia, SC
17 June 2020

11544585R00059